THE MODERN NATIONS IN
HISTORICAL PERSPECTIVE

ROBIN W. WINKS, *General Editor*

The idea of the nation state, which has dominated Europe since the French Revolution, now serves the entire globe. To the resultant profusion of political units the historian must bring perspective, both to re-emphasize the universal quality of nationhood and to help make clear the diversity and particularity of national experience.

The volumes in this series deal with individual nations or groups of closely related nations, summarizing the chief historical trends and influences that have contributed to each nation's present-day character, problems, and behavior. Recent data are incorporated with established historical background to achieve a fresh synthesis and original interpretation.

The author of this volume, ARTHUR P. WHITAKER, is Professor of Latin American History at the University of Pennsylvania. His interest in Latin America was inspired by study in Spain from 1924-6 as an Amherst Memorial Fellow. He is the author of many books, including *The United States and Argentina* (1954), *The Western Hemisphere Idea: Its Rise and Decline* (1954), *Argentine Upheaval: Perón's Fall and the New Regime* (1956), and *Spain and Defense of the West* (1961).

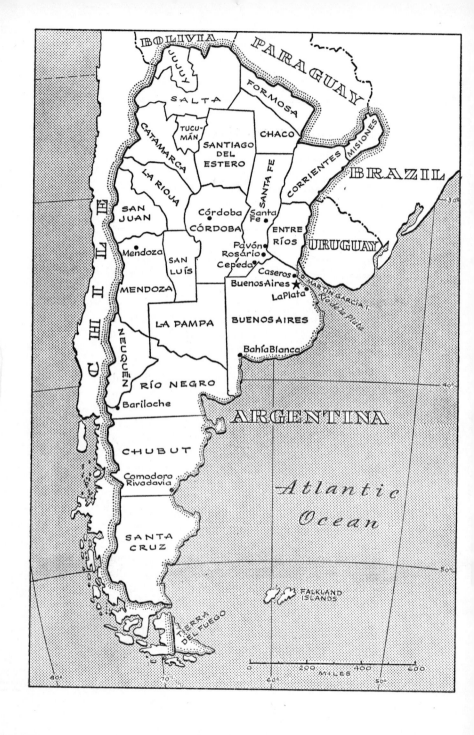

ARGENTINA

ARTHUR P. WHITAKER

A SPECTRUM BOOK

Prentice-Hall, Inc.

Englewood Cliffs, New Jersey

PREFACE

In accordance with the general plan of the series to which it belongs, this book is focused on the twentieth century. Two of its nine chapters, however, deal with the nineteenth-century beginnings of the Argentine nation and of conflicts that still agitate it today, such as those between democracy and authoritarianism, nativism and cosmopolitanism, centralization and decentralization, Buenos Aires and the provinces. Also, the nineteenth century would require attention if only because the contemporary phenomenon of Peronism has its main roots in a transformation of Argentine society that began in full force about 1880 and was started even earlier.

Although the history of every country is in many ways unique, the century and a half of Argentine history covered in this book has wider applications. One of these—its arrested development—should be of special interest to students of the developing nations of Asia and Africa as well as Latin America. What the latter now aspire to was achieved by Argentina between 1880 and the World War of 1914: a miraculous economic development which, despite a population explosion, was accompanied by a dramatic rise in the standard of living and the literacy rate and by the strengthening of democracy. In the next generation an important industrial component was added to the agricultural-commercial base, and by 1940 the Argentine economy seemed to have reached the take-off point. Yet it has not to this day taken off, and the nation's development in political, social, and cultural ways has also bogged down. Hence the title of this book. It is to be hoped that the arrest is only temporary, for its causes are essentially political and hence can be corrected by the Argentine people—and by them alone—if they have the

v

will to correct them. They certainly have the intelligence, aptitudes, and natural resources.

For aid in dealing with various problems discussed in this book, I am indebted to Ricardo Caillet-Bois, Gino Germani, and José Luis Romero, Argentine consultants on the study of nationalism in Argentina which I have directed since 1959; to Joseph R. Barager, a member of the advisory committee for that study, who read the whole manuscript and made valuable suggestions for its improvement; to Otis H. Green and Howard Perkins, also members of the advisory committee; and to the following students, past or present, in my seminar on Argentine nationalism: Samuel L. Baily, Earl Glauert, Marvin Goldwert, David Jordan, James Levy, and Winthrop R. Wright.

A.P.W.

CONTENTS

ONE

Argentina Today

Argentina is a maverick. It does not fit into any of the common categories of nations, such as "underdeveloped" or "developed," and "democratic" or "authoritarian," and it does not even run true to any Latin American type. Yet its recent history resembles that of many underdeveloped nations of both hemispheres in a wide variety of ways, and perhaps most of all in the persistence of social ferment and political instability, in the rise of populistic nationalism, and in the expansion of the armed forces' role. In all these respects Argentina was a pioneer, for it entered upon the present cycle a third of a century ago.

What differentiates Argentina most sharply from the rest of the so-called Latin American group is, paradoxically, the fact that, except for tiny Uruguay, it is the only one whose ethnic composition warrants the term Latin: its present population is overwhelmingly Spanish or Italian in origin, with relatively little of the Negro, Indian, and mestizo* elements so strong in all the rest. And although Argentina is one of the "big three" of Latin America, it differs widely from the other two, Portuguese-speaking Brazil and largely mestizo Mexico. Its population, some 21 million, is much smaller than theirs and is growing less rapidly. On the other hand, Argentina is far ahead of the other two both culturally, as measured by rate of literacy, and economically, as measured by per capita income.

In fact, in every respect Argentina is so much further advanced

---

* Mestizo: mixed white and Indian.

1

than most nations of Latin America, Asia, and Africa that it is not underdeveloped in the same sense. Yet it is by no means fully developed, for it still lags far behind such countries as the United States, Canada, Great Britain, France, and West Germany. As a result, its present state of development is best described as "intermediate."

Similarly, on the basis of its recent history, Argentina cannot be assigned definitively to either the democratic or the authoritarian category. Since 1930 it has alternated between the two and has spent a decade under a regime, headed by Juan Perón, which combined features of both systems. In the latest phase, after a year and a half of thinly veiled military dictatorship, it returned once more, in 1963, to representative, constitutional democracy. Whether this will close the cycle of instability remains to be seen.

Argentina and World Problems

As the foregoing suggests, despite Argentina's many idiosyncrasies, it illustrates several contemporary problems of worldwide interest. Three of these will be sketched here; they have been chosen not only because of their outstanding importance today, but also because, at least in Argentina's case, they have deep roots in the past and bid fair to endure for many years to come.

The first is the problem of the development of underdeveloped countries. As is well known, though too often forgotten, this problem is not only economic but social, political, and cultural as well. Also, it is international and often involves, among other things, policy decisions in other countries besides those in process of development. A prime illustration today is the Alliance for Progress and the role of the United States in relation to it. The Alliance is based on the assumptions that the promotion of economic growth and social welfare can go hand in hand; that significant progress, so rapid that the term "revolution" is commonly used to describe it, can and should be made toward these goals within ten years; and that the result will be the consolidation of stable, democratic societies in the countries thus developed.

Argentina's experience does not support these assumptions. As later pages will show in detail, beginning about 1880 the country enjoyed for several decades a spectacularly rapid economic and cultural development that placed it in the forefront of Latin America in everything but sheer size. The results have been most disappointing. Democracy has grown weaker instead of stronger; military coups have upset governments at shorter and shorter intervals since 1930. In economic development Argentina had reached the take-off point by the 1940s, and yet to this day it has not taken off; on the contrary, since 1950 there has actually been a decline in its per capita gross national product (total of all goods and services).* And all the while Argentine society has been increasingly fragmented by tensions arising from the earlier rapid growth; these have been both cause and effect of the country's economic and political reverses. If economic development is indeed the main highway to democracy, Argentina's experience of the past third of a century shows that the road is much longer, rougher, and more devious than many proponents of this view seem to realize.

Contemporary Argentina also illustrates the global theme of "pannationalism" developed in a recent book by Hans Kohn.† "The garb of nationalism," he writes, "clothes on the one hand the human aspirations for equality and dignity and on the other hand the passion for power over others." Argentina has exhibited one or both of these aspects ever since the beginning of its independence in 1810, but Juan Perón gave them a new twist in the decade after 1945. Capitalizing on the unrest of Argentina's *descamisados*, or "shirtless" masses, he identified nationalism with social justice as well as with resistance to "capitalist imperialism" and with devotion to Argentina's own hegemonic aspirations. The product was an early specimen of the populistic nationalism so widespread in the world today. Despite Perón's fall his program still has many adherents in Argentina, but this is only one of several nationalist groups in that country; in fact, Argentina has become a showcase for the whole spectrum of contemporary pan-nationalism.

The third and last illustration is the strength in Argentina of the worldwide sentiment favoring noncommitment in the Cold War.

---

* In February 1962 President Frondizi, noting that Argentina's growth rate had been negative since 1950, warned that if it were maintained, by 1975 the present per capita income of $460 would be reduced to $420, whereas Brazil's at the current rate would rise from $230 to $511. (Felix Luna, *Diálogos con Frondizi*, p. 187.)

† *The Age of Nationalism. The First Era of Global History* (New York, 1962).

Although this has deep historic roots in Argentina's tradition of isolationism, it owes its current formulation mainly to Juan Perón, who gave it the label "Third Position." This he distinguished sharply from neutralism, which, he asserted, was too rigid and quite unrealistic in the modern world, whereas noncommitment permitted flexible participation in world affairs on terms compatible with Argentine national interests. Among the latter he identified the Third Position with populistic nationalism and so with social reform for the benefit of the masses. Partly for this very reason, certain Argentines have reacted strongly against the Third Position and in favor of full commitment to the West in the Cold War. They, too, can invoke tradition, for Argentina has always had internationalists as well as isolationists. It would be foolhardy to predict which policy will prevail in the years just ahead, for both sides are strong. Moreover, despite Perón's overthrow in 1955, his Third Position label not only retains its attractions for many Argentines but has also been adopted by elements in other Latin American countries, including some of the new Christian Democratic parties.

Land and People

Argentina has often been compared to the United States, and the two do have certain features in common, such as the open character of their society, the enterprising spirit of their people, the federal, republican system of their governments, rapid urbanization, and exceptionally heavy immigration from Europe for several decades before World War I. But they differ so greatly in number of inhabitants and other respects that perhaps a comparison with Canada would be more instructive. The populations of the two countries are about the same size (Argentina 21 million, Canada 18 million); both are thinly populated (19 persons per square mile in Argentina, and 5 in Canada, as compared with 46 in Mexico) and yet highly urbanized (about two thirds in both countries), and in both there are heavy concentrations in the eastern part of the country, on or near rivers emptying into the Atlantic: the Paraná-Plata and the St. Lawrence. Moreover, Argentina and Canada have been much alike in their economic development: both first became, and still are, large-scale exporters of foodstuffs, mainly to Europe; both then added a substantial degree of industrialization; and in both the whole process was greatly aided by foreign investments. Finally, the anti-United States feeling that developed so strongly in Canada in the 1950s had its prototype in Argentina.

Needless to say, these two countries differ in many ways. The most striking differences, Canada's more rapid economic development and greater political stability, are interrelated. In 1959, for example, when Argentina still derived 23 per cent of its national income from agriculture, as compared with only 20 per cent from manufacturing, the corresponding figures for Canada were 7 per cent and 26 per cent. By this time Canada's per capita income was four times as large as Argentina's; and the frustration of Argentine hopes for a similar growth has combined with profound disagreement among the Argentines over the means of achieving it to keep the country in a turmoil ever since 1930.

Unlike Canada, Argentina lies mainly in the temperate zone, though it stretches northward into the subtropics and southward past the Tierra del Fuego to the Antarctic. Its area is about equal to that of the United States east of the Mississippi. Large parts of it are in various stages of underdevelopment. The southern third of continental Argentina, Patagonia, has little but sheepraising. The north and west, which contain the oldest settlements in the country, dating from the sixteenth century, have made a partial recovery from the decline which began in the late colonial period; among their most thriving centers today are sugar-producing Tucumán in the far north, and Mendoza, focus of the wine industry, in the foothills of the Andes. But Argentina's main concentration of population, agriculture, manufacturing, and commerce lies on or near the Plata and Paraná rivers, in a zone some 400 miles long and 250 miles wide extending from the province of Buenos Aires northward to Córdoba.

The greatest concentration of all is in the city of Buenos Aires. In 1963 the city proper had an estimated population of 4 million and was, as it had been for several decades, the second largest city in the Western Hemisphere. In that year its whole metropolitan area, Greater Buenos Aires, contained seven million inhabitants, or one third of Argentina's total population. Though this degree of concentration is exceptionally high in comparison with other countries, it is not surprising, for Buenos Aires is not only the nation's political, economic, and cultural capital, but also has few equals in the world as a national transportation center. All the principal lines of Argentina's railway network (the largest in Latin America and seventh largest in the world) converge on Buenos Aires. So does most shipping, whether coastwise, river, or trans-Atlantic; and so, in lesser but still high degree, do the air lines.

No other city in Argentina approaches Buenos Aires in size. The second and third largest, Rosario and Córdoba, are respectively only one tenth and one twelfth as large. The disparity in both size and power between the capital city and the provincial centers long since gave rise to an antagonism that is still a major source of political trouble in Argentina. This antagonism has been intensified by the extraordinarily high proportion of foreigners in the population of Buenos Aires. From 50 per cent in 1895, this had been reduced to 26 per cent by 1947, mainly because, after 1930, a sharp decline in immigration from abroad was accompanied by a corresponding rise in migration from Argentina's own interior to Buenos Aires. Yet this internal migration has done little to alleviate the old antagonism between the capital city and the provinces. On the other hand, as will be shown in a later chapter, the newer problem of social tensions has been aggravated by the concentration of the in-migrants alongside the nation's main focus of wealth, gentility, and Europeanized culture, for most of the newcomers have been unskilled workers of humble origin and dark complexion, with an affinity for grass-roots Argentinism and xenophobia.

Although nationalism is widespread and deep-rooted in Argentina, the nationalists are divided among themselves and it is still true that, as one acute Argentine observer, José Luis Romero, wrote nearly two decades ago, the predominant characteristics and common traits of its people are difficult to identify, "for the collective personality of the country is still in proces of formation." Hence even data that have the reassuring appearance of statistical accuracy can be interpreted in various ways. For what they may be worth, some of these data are noted here.*

The Argentines are the best-fed people in the Western Hemisphere; in daily caloric intake (3,360 calories) they are ahead of the United

* Most of the data following are drawn from *Statistical Abstract of Latin America 1962*, prepared by the Center of Latin American Studies, University of California, Los Angeles.

States (3,100) and Canada (3,070) and far ahead of most of Latin America. Their reputation as meat-eaters is well earned, though in this respect they fall behind Uruguay, the United States, and Canada. They stand at or near the top of the Hemisphere nations in health facilities, with more physicians and dentists, in proportion to population, than even the United States, and more hospital beds than any Latin American country except Costa Rica. In life expectancy, 57 years at birth for males, Argentina leads all the Hemisphere nations except Panama, the United States, and Canada; the corresponding rates in the other largest Latin American countries, Mexico and Brazil, are 38 and 39 years. And yet the rate of population increase in Argentina (1.9 per cent per year) is well below that in most Latin American countries, including Mexico and Brazil. So is Argentina's proportion of children under 15 to total population (about 30 per cent, compared with 40 per cent or more in Brazil, Mexico, and most of the rest). Conversely Argentina's proportion of persons in the most productive age group, 20 to 64, is the highest in Latin America.

Argentina also stands first or second in Latin America in book production and in newspaper circulation and the number of telephones and radio sets in proportion to population; in the number of television sets it stands third, after Brazil and Mexico. It leads all but Uruguay in literacy (about 87 per cent) and is far ahead in the ratio of university students to population. Yet only one seventh of its population of school age continues beyond the primary grades, and only one twentieth reaches the university level. Even so, the six national universities are badly overcrowded; the student-teacher ratio (27 to 1) is much the highest in Latin America; and the share of the national budget allotted to education is low on the Latin American scale—in 1959 it stood last by a narrow margin.

In religious affiliation, the census of 1947 showed that 93.6 per cent of the Argentine people were Roman Catholics, 2 per cent Protestants, and 1.8 per cent of no faith. In addition, Argentina contains far more Jews than any other Latin American country; in 1963 they were said to number 450,000. Of the overwhelmingly Roman Catholic majority, it is commonly said that only 10 or 15 per cent are "practicing," but it is doubtful whether such estimates are useful clues to behavior. Priests are proportionately more numerous than in the other largest Latin American countries: one to 4,100 Catholics in

Argentina, as compared with one to 4,800 in Mexico and one to 5,550 in Brazil.

Argentina has produced men of international distinction in various fields, such as the nineteenth-century jurist Carlos Calvo and two of Latin America's three Nobel Prize winners, Carlos Saavedra Lamas (1936), the peace prize, and Bernardo A. Houssay (1947), the prize in medicine and physiology. Despite the assorted vicissitudes through which the country has passed in recent decades, the quality of its intellectual elite remains at a high level. Leadership now comes mainly from the fragmented middle class rather than, as formerly, from the upper class—a fact which may help to explain the great diversity of outlook and interest that characterizes the present generation of intellectual leaders. Some of them, for example, are deeply concerned with public affairs, as were nearly all their predecessors, while others apparently could not care less.

Among the latter are two of the handful of Argentine writers who are highly esteemed abroad as well as at home. These are Jorge Luis Borges, born in 1899, author of fantastic tales and regarded by critics as one of the best stylists in any country, and Julio Cortázar, a younger writer of the same school. Midway in this respect stands Argentina's outstanding novelist, Eduardo Mallea, who divides his time between ivory tower and forum. Those who have been fully committed include such notables as the late Francisco Romero, one of Latin America's best known philosophers; his brother, José Luis Romero, intellectual historian, university official, and long an active Socialist; and Ezequiel Martínez Estrada, astringent critic of Argentine society and its two conflicting traditions, identified in Sarmiento's classic book of 1845 as civilization and barbarism. The conflict between these two traditions still goes on. So does the conflict over their redefinition; one of the major tasks of Argentina's committed intellectuals today is to reconcile them in a national synthesis. But more of this later.

Government and Parties

Argentina is still governed under its Constitution of 1853, which is the oldest now in force in Latin America. Modelled rather closely on that of the United States, it is nominally federal. Today, however, Argentina's government is marked by an even greater concentration

of power in the central government, and especially in the presidency:
in the central government, because of its constitutional right, frequently exercised, to intervene in the provinces; and in the presidency
because, in addition to possessing all the powers of the president
of the United States, the Argentine president can summon and dis-
solve Congress, govern by decree-laws, and suspend constitutional
guarantees by declaring a "state of siege." Another difference is that
the Argentine constitution requires the government to support the
Roman Catholic Church and makes only members of that church
eligible for the presidency; but it guarantees freedom of worship for
all other faiths, and this stipulation has always been enforced.

Voting has been compulsory since 1910 and all adult women as
well as men have been eligible to vote since 1947. In the national
election of July 1963 the number of eligible voters was 11.5 million,
or slightly more than half the total population; of these, 9.3 million,
or 84 per cent, cast ballots.

Never very successful, the effort to develop a two-party system
under the Saenz Peña Law of 1912 was abandoned in 1963 in favor
of proportional representation. This gave a further stimulus to the
multiplication of parties, and the whole situation is complicated by
social and political tensions which since 1945 have related mainly to
Peronism. As a result, there is disunity everywhere. About half the
Argentine voters, most of them middle-class, are Radicals, but since
1957 they have been almost evenly divided into two quite separate
and mutually hostile parties, the Intransigent Radicals and the
Popular Radicals; and in the 1963 election the Intransigents split
again. There are also divisions among the next-largest group, the
Peronists, who number upwards of one fourth of the voters and are
supported mainly by organized labor. For several years after Perón's
flight they showed a high degree of unity under his absentee management, but this was less apparent in the election of 1962 and vanished
in the election of 1963. Even the splinter parties are split. This is
true of the old Socialists as well as of the new Christian Democrats,
products of the 1890s and the 1950s respectively. The conservatives,
who long monopolized the government, have been reduced to a loose
and weak Confederation of Parties of the Center.

The resulting fragmentation was faithfully reflected in the outcome of the presidential election of July 1963. The four top parties'

combined popular vote was only 76 per cent of the total; the winner, Popular Radical Arturo Illia, polled only 26 per cent; and 21 parties elected one or more members of the Electoral College. Consequently, Illia achieved the necessary 51 per cent majority in the Electoral College only by obtaining the votes of four minor parties. The same election gave seats to 24 parties in the approximately 200-member Chamber of Deputies, in which formerly five or six parties at most had been represented; and Illia's victorious Popular Radicals fell some 20 seats short of winning a majority.

The problem of Peronism continues to haunt Argentina. In its present form this problem arises from the fact that more than one fourth of the people remain loyal to the exiled Perón or (which is not necessarily the same thing) to Peronism. Although their strength lies mainly in the organized labor movement, it also includes some middle-class elements. To them, Perón's overthrow represented a right-wing reaction both against the "social conquests" made by the masses, and also against the progress toward economic independence made by the whole nation, under his regime. The Peronists are determined to protect (or recover) and enlarge these gains. To this end they demand treatment as first-class citizens, with the right to organize their own parties. Many non-Peronists support this demand, both on the abstract ground of justice and on the practical ground that national reconciliation, peace, and progress cannot be achieved in any other way. On the other hand, there are likewise many Argentines, spearheaded by military elements but including good democrats among the civilians, who bitterly oppose any concession to the Peronists, on the grounds that they are antidemocratic, tainted with Communism and Castroism, and aiming at the restoration of the Peronist system and even of Perón himself.

The conflict over this issue has been a major source of discord ever since Perón's fall. It has been complicated, and in some measure tempered, by the fact, already noted, that the Peronists have been permitted to vote, for some of the legal parties scrambled for their votes, which were largely controlled by the exiled Perón. The scramble was led by Intransigent Radical Arturo Frondizi, whose success in the enterprise first made him president and then unmade him: elected president with the aid of Peronist votes in 1958, he was ousted by the military in 1962, mainly on the ground that he was too soft on

Peronism. In the latest phase, opened by the election of 1963, this issue remains unresolved, as do the other major issues.*

Power Groups

Argentina's near future depends mainly on the country's two principal power groups, the armed forces and organized labor. Since neither is a monolithic unit, their behavior is difficult to predict. The armed forces number about 112,000 (85,000 in the army, 21,000 in the navy, and 6,000 in the air force), with another 250,000 in the trained reserve; they are roughly one half as large as Brazil's, one third as large as Mexico's, and twice as large as Chile's. Their political orientation is, not unnaturally, determined mainly by their officers. These were formerly tied to the oligarchy and some still are, but in recent years the greater part of them have maintained the outlook of the middle class, from which they come, with all the disunity and confusion inherent in that fact. Quite recently, however, at least the majority of them seem to have lined up in favor of constitutional democracy. Successive purges from Perón's time to the present have apparently disillusioned them with the political role that the armed forces began to play in 1930 and have convinced them that, after all, politics are not too important to be left to the civilians.

To be sure, there are still "Nasserists" † and other political activists among the military and it is still too early to say whether the current nonpolitical mood will continue to prevail. It is certainly contrary to the trend in other Latin American countries, where the political role of the military has been greatly expanded in recent years. There is, however, nothing surprising about the contrast, for Argentina has often either departed from or anticipated the line of development in the rest of Latin America.

Yet even if the current mood of the Argentine armed forces does last, it will continue to require three qualifications. The first is that their abstention from political activity is not unconditional, and they would almost certainly not permit the establishment of a Peronist or Communist regime. In the second place, there is no prospect that they will give up either their time-honored and hence "normal"

* For a discussion of this election, see Chapter Nine.
† Advocates of authoritarian nationalism based on an alliance between the armed forces and the workers; named for the Egyptian Nasser.

participation in governments through cabinet appointments (these always include the military ministries, and sometimes others, particularly Interior, or *Gobierno*, and Foreign Affairs), or their substantial share of the national budget, which in 1959 amounted to 15 per cent of the total budget, as compared with 26 per cent in Brazil, 12.7 per cent in Chile, and 11.1 per cent in Mexico. Third and finally, the Argentine military are more likely to increase than to diminish the "civic action" which they have developed on a large scale in recent decades. This has given them a very important role in nonpolitical aspects of the nation's life, especially the economic aspect, through military participation in the planning and direction of such enterprises as the government petroleum agency, Yacimientos Petrolíferos Fiscales or Y.P.F., and the San Nicolás steel plant.

Organized labor is best represented by the General Confederation of Labor (C.G.T.), made up of 135 unions of widely assorted sizes whose total membership is about 2.5 million. Well over half the members belong to a group of Peronist unions, and about one third to an independent or democratic group. The rest are Communist-controlled. The three groups are called respectively "the 62," "the 32," and "the 19," from the original number of unions in each. Although the differentiation between the two main groups as regards white-collar workers (*empleados*) and blue-collar or no-collar workers (*obreros*) is not at all clear-cut, more of the former are found in the independent unions and more of the latter in the Peronist unions. Some of the largest unions in the two groups are, among the Peronists, textile, metallurgical, and *frigorífico* (meat packing plant) workers; among the independents, the railway brotherhood, government workers, and commercial employees.

These groups have functioned separately to such an extent ever since 1955 that the unity of the C.G.T. has often been merely nominal. It may become much more real under the definitive plan of reorganization adopted in February 1963, after five years of government intervention followed by two years of provisional administration. The reorganization gave the Peronists firm control of the C.G.T. They also shaped its platform, which contained such features as demands for worker participation in the control of business enterprises, full employment, price ceilings on essential commodities, and agrarian reform, and a condemnation of Argentina's participation in the blockade of Cuba during the crisis of October 1962 over Soviet missiles. Disagreement between the independent and Peronist groups on such matters relates more often to procedure than to policy. Thus, the Peronist unions have generally been much more aggressive, particularly in advocating the use of the general strike as a political weapon, and more than once such strikes have been frustrated by the independents, who generally oppose the identification of organized labor with any political party. On specific political issues, most of which were omitted from the C.G.T. platform, the differences usually are much wider, but even here the dividing line is often blurred or crossed.

There are, of course, many lesser but still important opinion-forming or action groups that must be taken into account. These include, for example, associations of businessmen, bankers, and manufacturers which play a major role in their respective fields; but after nearly four years in the presidency, Frondizi complained that the public welfare suffered because there was no one central organization that could speak for business and the employers as the C.G.T. was speaking for labor. The Roman Catholic Church in Argentina has spoken with more than one voice in Argentina in recent years. As a body, the hierarchy has followed its usual course of remaining aloof from political controversy, while at the same time, in the spirit of Pope John XXIII's encyclical *Mater et Magistra*, it has asserted its right and duty to speak out on social questions. Some members of the clergy, high as well as low, have given aid and comfort to the Peronist cause in the name of social justice. At the opposite extreme, others have identified themselves with the radical right; an outstanding example is Father Julio Meinvielle, who has been writing in an antidemocratic, anti-Semitic vein for many years and has recently become an adviser to a Nazi-type youth organization called Tacuara.

The Argentine press is, of course, a Tower of Babel, with as many different voices as there are editors and financial backers, but the older and (to the outside world) better known newspapers have not dealt gently with the pulling and hauling among Peronists, Frondizists, and the military. Often, they have spoken for a large body of public opinion in saying, "A plague on all your houses." As for the intellectuals, there is a dangerous ferment among the thousands of unemployed teachers and briefless lawyers turned out by the country's universities and institutes. But, moving higher up the scale, to those intellectuals who have arrived in one way or another, we find in even greater degree the diversity of outlook and opinion already noted in other sectors of Argentine society.

As seen by foreign observers, the intellectuals' one common trait, which is also a fault, is their preoccupation with what went wrong —with, so to speak, Argentina's misspent youth. Even so fine and versatile a novelist as Eduardo Mallea devoted a whole book, *La vida blanca*, to describing the Argentine people's moral and spiritual decline; written in the depressing circumstances of 1942, this book was prudently withheld from publication for many years, but finally published as still valid in 1960. It is true that this preoccupation with what went wrong is to some extent bound up with a historical revisionism that turns the orthodox account of Argentina's past upside down, so that along with the debunking there is also rehabilitation. The total effect, however, remains negative. There is much truth in the observation, made in 1962 by a Spanish visitor to Argentina who knows the country well: "These members of [Argentina's] new intellectual and professional middle class who have so roundly abused its now-defunct oligarchy have never themselves been able to provide leadership in public affairs."

The current state of affairs in Argentina has the depressing effect of any confusion. Yet it also has a hopeful aspect, for the multiple thrusts and counterthrusts tend to cancel each other out and open the way for positive action by those who have recently come to power. The latter are also favored by what seems to be the prevalent national mood, compounded of relief that an abyss has been avoided and determination not to skirt it again. They will need all the help they can get, for grave problems still face the country. Nevertheless, the odds are at least slightly in their favor if they meet the challenge with imagination and constancy.

International Relations

Argentina's foreign relations are in a state of flux. Nominally, her traditional political policy of modified isolationism has been abandoned since 1945. First under Perón, then under Provisional President Pedro Aramburu and President Arturo Frondizi, Argentina joined the United Nations and the restructured Organization of American States, ratified the Inter-American Treaty of Reciprocal Assistance (Rio Defense Pact), joined the Paris Club, the World Bank and the International Monetary Fund (IMF), and finally, in 1958, signed a stabilization agreement with the IMF. She thereby not only assumed both general and specifically American regional obligations with regard to the maintenance of international peace and security, and aligned herself with the West in the Cold War, but also tied her hands with respect to her own domestic financial and economic policy.

Yet Argentina's attitude toward these commitments remains ambiguous and uncertain. This is partly because they are strongly opposed by many Argentines, and partly because even the authorities responsible for making them had mental reservations or second thoughts. It seems clear that both Perón and Frondizi made commitments of this kind as a matter of practical necessity, mainly in order to obtain badly needed aid from the United States and Western Europe, and that deep down, both men preferred the flexible policy of noncommitment that Perón labelled "Third Position." * A specific illustration of the uncertainty of Argentina's Western trumpet was Frondizi's refusal in 1961-62 to join in inter-American enforcement measures against Castro Cuba, despite the latter's threat to inter-American security and open affiliation with the Communist bloc of nations. Another illustration is the fact that the platform of the winner of the presidential election in 1963, Arturo Illia, called for the cancellation of the stabilization agreement and withdrawal from the International Monetary Fund, so as to recover Argentina's freedom in fiscal and economic policy. Such attitudes reflect powerful forces of nationalism, mass ferment, and a bias against the United States. Yet they are opposed by other strong elements in the country who maintain that, in its own national interest, Argentina must confirm and strengthen its commitment to international cooperation and alignment with the West. The election of 1963 did not settle this conflict over foreign policy, and in view of the strength of the

* As noted above, Perón also applied this term to his domestic policy. It is further discussed, with Justicialism, in Chapter Seven.

contending groups and the fragmentation of Argentine society, a definitive settlement of it may not be reached for some years to come.

Argentina still maintains important cultural and economic relations with the outside world, especially with Western Europe. Since 1940 the United States has displaced Great Britain as the principal foreign investor in Argentina, and its influence has grown in the business and industrial sectors. Beginning under Perón, for example, Kaiser Industries has achieved a leading position in Argentina's automobile industry, and under Frondizi, after 1958, U.S. firms aided greatly in the expansion of petroleum production. There has also been some growth of educational influence, as, for example, through the establishment of a cooperative arrangement between Columbia University and the University of Buenos Aires. In addition, earlier ties between the two countries still exist, such as the operation of U.S. banks in Argentina, the use by Argentines of U.S. newsgathering services, and the citation of U.S. judicial opinions by Argentine courts and lawyers in interpreting their Constitution of 1853.

On the whole, however, the North Americanization of Argentina, recommended a century ago by one of that country's leading statesmen, Domingo F. Sarmiento, has made very limited progress. What is more, its further progress seems doubtful in view of recent economic and social trends and the prevailing climate of opinion in the two countries. A modern industrial society is developing in Argentina, but insofar as this does not assume the "autochthonous character" demanded by Argentina's omnipresent nationalists, it is more likely to resemble the Western European models that have been emerging since World War II, for these are more compatible with the Argentine trend toward a combination of capitalism with socialism and of free enterprise with government control. Although Argentina's traditional European bias has been weakened since World War I by the rise of nationalism and other factors, in recent years Western Europe's prestige among the Argentines has waxed again as a result both of its remarkable recovery since 1950 and also of Argentina's reverses, which have somewhat diminished its people's confidence in themselves.

European cultural influence in Argentina, though manifestly great, cannot be measured statistically, but Western Europe's likewise great commercial importance to Argentina can. It accounts for one half of Argentina's total foreign trade, and its share is three times as large as that of the United States. The discrepancy is even greater when Argentine exports alone are considered, for Europe provides a far larger market than does the United States for Argentina's exports, which consist mainly of meat and grains; here the ratio is about eight to one in favor of Europe. Great Britain is still, as always, Argentina's best customer, though by a narrower margin than before World War II. It now takes about 20 per cent of Argentina's total exports, but as a group the European Common Market countries' share is twice as large as Britain's. Consequently, the Argentines are deeply disturbed by the prospect that this trade will be crippled by the adoption of Common Market measures giving preferred treatment to the agricultural products of the member countries and their former dependencies outside Europe (principally the former French colonies in Africa). The prospect would be even worse, of course, if Britain joined the Common Market; hence the great rejoicing on the banks of the Plata when, early in 1963, General de Gaulle decreed Britain's exclusion from it.

This situation has spurred Argentina to great efforts to find new markets for its export products. Since these are almost wholly agricultural and pastoral, the possibilities are limited, and so far the results have not been encouraging. Trade pacts or other arrangements have been made with Communist bloc countries, but these account for only five per cent of Argentina's total trade. The volume of trade with Asia (mainly Japan and India) is slightly larger, but Argentina's imports exceed her exports, and the latter are only about one fourth as large as to Great Britain alone. Argentine exports to Oceania and Africa are microscopic. The United States is still looked to as a potentially large market for Argentine meat, but most of this is still excluded under a sanitary regulation aimed against the hoof-and-mouth disease and first adopted in 1926. In order to reach this market, Argentine authorities are attempting to stamp out the hoof-and-mouth disease in their country, and in the meantime to develop processing techniques that will enable their beef to take the hurdle of the sanitary regulation.

Naturally, Argentina's search for new markets has also been conducted nearer home, in Latin America. In this connection its government joined with five other South American countries and Mexico in establishing in 1960 the Latin American Free Trade Association. LAFTA represented an imitation of Europe as well as a defensive reaction against the European Common Market, but its model was the looser Free Trade Association composed of Great Britain and six continental countries. It aimed not at complete integration but at stimulating intra-Latin American trade through lowering tariff barriers, and this was to be done gradually over a ten-year period. Down to the present (1963), its accomplishments have been equally modest. Argentina's trade with the other LAFTA members has grown only slightly since 1960 and still amounts to less than 10 per cent of its total trade. Its trade with Latin American countries not belonging to LAFTA is very small except in the case of Venezuela, and even this is declining since it consists mainly of imports of Venezuelan oil, which are diminishing as Argentina increases her own petroleum production.

For Argentina, as for its other members, LAFTA also differs from the European Common Market in another respect: ostensibly it is a purely economic arrangement, without the latter's implications of political union. Yet despite official disclaimers, LAFTA almost certainly does have such political implications, at least in the minds of influential Argentines, including Arturo Frondizi, who, as President of Argentina at the time of LAFTA's creation, was one of its principal backers. LAFTA is intended to include all Latin America ultimately, and its Argentine promoters are well aware that economic union can be a prelude to political union. But even if it goes no further than economic union—and even that is, to be sure, a long-range goal—it will have three merits in their eyes. First, it will increase their bargaining power in international markets. As Frondizi told an audience in Chile in April 1958, economic cooperation among the Latin American nations should be aimed not only at promoting their trade with one another, but also at "defending" the prices of their products in the world market. In the second place, it will give them the sense of belonging to a substantial community, and thus will relieve the distress many of them have long suffered from the feeling that they are isolated, second-class members of the Western world. If you can't lick them, join them, is an old adage; to which the corollary is, if you can't join them, form a club of your own.

Finally, the development of a "Latin American community" is an old dream in Argentina as well as in other countries south of the Rio Grande, and its realization today is regarded by many people in Argentina as the renewal of a great tradition too long forgotten, or, if not forgotten, at least little noted by most Argentine statesmen for more than a century past.

TWO

FROM COLONY TO REPUBLIC

1810-1880

The establishment of Argentine independence was one phase of the disintegration of Spain's American empire between 1810 and 1825. That process in turn belongs to the anticolonial phase of the Atlantic world's age of revolution, which began in 1776 with the American Revolution, continued with the French Revolution, and then, after several decades of upheavals on both sides of the Atlantic, spent itself in Europe's revolutionary outburst of 1848-49.

When it ended, Argentina was still passing through the era of domestic strife and dictatorship which was the common lot of the new Spanish American states after independence. Also, Argentine society still retained in many ways the colonial character formed during nearly three centuries of Spanish rule. There were a few towns and cities, topped by cosmopolitan Buenos Aires and the citadel of Catholicism, Córdoba, but as late as 1869 (the first census), three fourths of the population was rural. At midcentury Argentina was still essentially a cow country in which wild cattle were slaughtered for their hides by wilder men of a cowboy type called *gauchos*. Efforts to modernize this society on European and North American models had begun with independence, but they were so stoutly resisted by traditionalists that for a generation they only complicated the struggle for unity and order.

This struggle continued with hardly a let-up until 1880. When it was over, the modernizers had won and Argentina stood on the threshold of a transformation that was soon to make it the richest, most dynamic, and most Europeanized country in Latin America, but which also sowed the seeds of future discord. Also, out of that seventy-year-long struggle emerged a varied assortment of leaders who served later generations as representatives of contrasting Argentine types: on the one hand, traditionalists such as Facundo Quiroga, provincial *caudillo* or chieftain, and Juan Manuel de Rosas, forerunner of Juan Perón; and on the other hand, builders of the new Argentina, such as Domingo Faustino Sarmiento, Juan Bautista Alberdi, and Bartolomé Mitre. In between these two types, and in a sense linking them, was the Liberator, General José de San Martín, sometimes called the George Washington of Argentina.

Argentine writers have summed up the whole period from 1810 to 1880 as a quest for national self-identification. In general terms this meant the determination of the new state's political, economic, and social system and its geographical extent. The quest involved a protracted conflict over concrete issues between such opposing forces as those of centralization and decentralization, authoritarianism and democracy, traditionalism and modernization, clericalism and anticlericalism. The main outlines of the conflict are sketched in the present chapter. The story falls into two main parts divided by the adoption of the liberal, federal Constitution of 1853, which represented both a major policy decision and a compromise; it settled some issues but left unresolved others which continued to plague the country until 1880.

FORCES OF UNION AND DISUNION, 1810-1853

Between the beginning of independence in 1810 and the compromise of 1853 Argentina passed through a time of troubles similar in some ways to that which has afflicted the country since 1930. In both periods protracted strife was followed by the establishment of authoritarian, nationalistic regimes resting on a broad base of popular support but strongly opposed by many Argentines, including most intellectuals, and finally overthrown by their own armed forces. Perhaps the most striking difference between the two periods is that, whereas the earlier one was marked by progress toward a national consensus as to what Argentina was and ought to be, since 1930 the trend has been in the opposite direction. How and why the reversal took place will be shown in later chapters.

Progress toward a national consensus in the first two generations of the new republic's life resulted from the interplay among variegated and often conflicting forces at work among a sparse population (numbering about 700,000 in 1820) scattered over a great expanse of territory. This stretched from the mouth of the Plata River in the Atlantic to the eastern slopes of the Andes and from the borderland of the plains Indians near Buenos Aires northward to the Bolivian frontier. The conflict is often oversimplified by describing it as one between the port city of Buenos Aires and the hinterland. Cosmopolitan Buenos Aires, we are told, advocated centralization and modernization on the model of France and England and at the expense of the inherited and modified Spanish culture, whereas the traditionalist, particularistic hinterland and its local *caudillos* (leaders) were generally cool or hostile to such change and resisted the hegemonic pretensions of Buenos Aires.

This simplistic view has some merit and can be helpful as a guide through the maze of Argentina's early history, but it must be qualified if it is not to mislead. For one thing, Buenos Aires favored national union only on its own terms, and when these were not met it became the paladin of particularism. Moreover, the edges of the Buenos Aires–hinterland dichotomy were blurred in many ways, particularly as a result of two processes: first, beginning in the late colonial period, the multiplication of economic and personal as well as political ties between the two after the establishment of the Viceroyalty of La Plata in 1776; and second, after 1810, the mingling of troops drawn from various parts of the country and fighting in a common cause during the war for independence.

In the first stage of national development from 1810 to 1829, independence was declared and secured, the ideals and objectives of the new state were formulated in the so-called "May Doctrine," and its territorial limits were defined with some precision, but every effort at self-government failed. In 1829 the tyrant Rosas began his rise to power. The choice of 1810 as a starting-point is rather arbitrary, for, on the one hand, independence was not formally declared until July 9, 1816, and on the other hand, a national spirit began to take shape in 1806, when the Argentines, without help from Spain, repulsed a

British invasion. This feat was celebrated in a poem titled "The Argentine Triumph" (*El triunfo argentino*), which helped to popularize and invest with political significance the hitherto purely literary term "Argentine."

Yet most Argentines date their country's independence from 1810 (its first centenary was officially celebrated in 1910), and the choice is defensible on two grounds. The first is that on May 25 of that year a town meeting (*cabildo abierto*) in Buenos Aires set up an autonomous government to function during the interregnum resulting from Napoleon's intervention in Spain; though this was nominally only a caretaker government and loyal to the Spanish crown, it led straight to independence. In the second place, the May Doctrine, which has been an article of faith with subsequent generations of Argentines, takes its name from pronouncements made in this same month of May; as later modified, notably in 1813, it is essentially the doctrine of a free and open society, but even authoritarians, such as Rosas and Perón, have paid lip service to it. From this same period comes the definition of Argentina's territory as coinciding with that of the colonial Viceroyalty of Buenos Aires, which included (in modern terms) Uruguay, Paraguay, and southern Bolivia as well as Argentina. The other parts soon broke away, but the belief that they should rightfully be united (or reunited) with Argentina has persisted in that country to our own times.

Military Success

In the first two decades after 1810 Argentina's leaders were mainly concerned with military and political problems. Those of an economic character were less pressing. To a large extent the country's economy was of the subsistence type, unresponsive to outside events and untouched by the war. For the rest, those sectors that relied on foreign trade and credit enjoyed the ministrations of foreigners, especially the British, who, ruling the waves, brooked no interference from any belligerents and whom most Argentines, forgetting or forgiving the invasion of 1806, welcomed with open arms. On the other hand, the military and political problems facing the new state were crucially important. Its leaders were far more successful in handling the former than the latter. Let us begin with the success story.

Although the outlying parts of the old viceroyalty—modern Paraguay, Uruguay, and southern Bolivia—were soon lost to Argentina, they were also lost to Spain, and the latter never reconquered either Buenos Aires or any substantial part of the Argentine hinterland. Spain did continue to offer a potential threat for a short time from Uruguay and for a longer time from Bolivia and Spain itself, but the potential was never realized. Another danger came from Brazil, first under Portuguese rule and then, after 1822, as an independent Empire. Both governments claimed Uruguay, occupied it for a time, and otherwise meddled in River Plate affairs, to the distress of Argentina. Hence the Argentine-Brazilian war of 1825-28, which weakened both countries and ended in a stalemate; but by that time the Spanish peril had ceased to exist.

From 1817 to 1822, despite the danger to their right flank and rear, the Argentines carried the war to Spain in Chile and Peru. They first aided mightily in the liberation of Chile and then began the liberation of Peru, Spain's last citadel on the American mainland. On both occasions, the hero was José de San Martín. A native of Argentina, San Martín had begun his career as an officer in the Spanish army and had served in the campaigns against Napoleon's forces in Spain. In 1812, however, he returned to fight for his country's independence. His most famous exploit was his carefully prepared crossing of the snow-clad Andes from Mendoza to Chile in 1817 with a force of some 5,000 soldiers which enabled the Chilean patriots to win their independence the following year. Unable either to complete the liberation of Peru without the aid of his Colombian counterpart, Simón Bolívar, or to get him to agree on terms of cooperation, San Martín retired in Bolívar's favor in 1822. Two years later, unwilling to try to cope with the chaotic political situation in Argentina, he left for France, where he died in 1850.

San Martín lacked the charismatic qualities that might have made him a popular hero in his own day, but he possessed other attributes which, long after his death, turned him into a symbol of Argentine nationalism—an odd quirk of fate, since his sympathies were broadly American rather than merely national. The explanation is important for an understanding of the Argentine people. It may lie in the combination of his exploits in the Argentine service during a heroic age with his possession of characteristics that Argentines admire at a distance, such as prudence, moderation, and tolerance. Though a free-mason and a monarchist at heart, he had no trouble in working with devout Catholics and fervent democrats. Even liberals laud this professional soldier, because he held that the armed forces should serve, not control, the government. "The army," he is quoted as saying, "is a lion that must be kept in a cage and not let out until the day of battle." His most controversial act was the bequeathing of his sword to the tyrant Rosas, but this was clearly done as a tribute, not to the tyrant, but to the defender of Argentina against French and British aggression.

Political Failure

In contrast with San Martín's exploits in Chile and Peru, every effort to organize Argentina domestically in the period to 1829 ended in frustration and failure. One reason for the difference may have been that San Martín's task was primarily military, that he had been trained for it, and that military authority and discipline made it relatively easy to reach decisions and carry them out. None of the many civilian leaders had had significant political experience, and the fundamental principles of independence handicapped all these efforts to organize the new state by limiting and diffusing authority and placing the protection of individual rights above the corporate interests of society.

Such a system might have worked if a substantial national consensus had existed in Argentina as it did in England and the United States, but that was not the case. There were Argentine nationalists from the start—the national anthem still sung by Argentines dates from 1813—but they were few and had little to build on but an idea. As a political unit, Argentina was completely new; so also, to its people, was the republican form of government; neither had a counterpart or precedent in the colonial period. Most of the loyalties, bonds of interest, and habits of cooperation that hold a nation together remained to be created when independence was declared. The common effort of the war for independence was of some help, but it ended long before unity was achieved. The United States faced a somewhat similar problem in its early years, but its leaders were far more experienced and its society more highly integrated, and there was no other independent power in North America to muddy its waters as neighboring South American states, notably Brazil, did in the case of Argentina.

In addition, many of the leaders of this period, from Mariano Moreno and Bernardo Monteagudo at the beginning to Bernardino Rivadavia in the 1820s, were doctrinaire rationalists who tried to reshape Argentine society forthwith on foreign models drawn mainly from the eighteenth-century Enlightenment and the French Revolution, thereby alienating conservatives and traditionalists. Theoretically these principles were admirable and they formed the core of the May Doctrine, which ultimately gained general acceptance; but that did not happen until after the doctrine had been made less rational and more realistic by adapting it to the conditions of life in Argentina.

Measures taken by the Assembly of 1813 strengthened the liberal content of the May Doctrine but thereby increased the turmoil of this period. In what we may describe as an effort to promote representative democracy by creating an open society, the Assembly decreed the abolition of entailed estates (*mayorazgos*), placed curbs on the powers of the Roman Catholic Church, freed the Indians from their badge of serfdom, the payment of tribute, and put Negro slavery in the way of extinction. If these and other measures of the same kind had been carried out, they would have brought about a social and economic revolution. Some of them were, but only after a long interval: Negro slavery was not abolished until the 1850s. Others were ignored or circumvented: the concentration of landowning in the hands of a small minority has continued in Argentina down to the present time. On the other hand, the reaction against the Assembly's sweeping reforms was instantaneous. They offended influential groups in all parts of the country but particularly in the interior provinces, for they bore the stamp of Buenos Aires, which was always suspect in the eyes of good provincials. As a concession to this antagonism, the congress that declared independence in 1816 was held at Tucumán, in northern Argentina.

Political instability was further aggravated by other problems, such as those presented by José Artigas, patriot leader of Uruguay, who successfully resisted its unification with Argentina. Governments continued to rise and fall in rapid succession and one lasted only three months.

In 1820 the revelation that the government had tried to establish a monarchy under a European prince provoked a revolution that brought the country to the verge of anarchy. Throughout most of the year all semblance of national unity disappeared. The provincial caudillos reigned supreme; some of them invaded each other's provinces; and in some of the provinces local civil wars broke out. One such province, that of Buenos Aires, had three rival governors at the same time.

When a measure of peace and order was restored near the end of the year, the decentralizers or Federals (*federales*) had won. Only the loosest kind of confederation remained. In effect, it was held together by a system of interprovincial pacts, and the few functions of a central government, which included little more than the conduct of foreign relations, were delegated to the provincial government of Buenos Aires.

Yet the opposite group, the centralizers or Unitarians (*unitarios*), pushed on undismayed under the leadership of Bernardino Rivadavia, a talented creole* with extensive diplomatic experience in Europe, who held a key government post in the keystone province, Buenos Aires. They had their hour of triumph when the Constitution of 1826 provided for a highly centralized government controlled by the elite through restrictions on the suffrage, and Rivadavia was elected president.

The Unitarians' triumph was brief, for Rivadavia quickly aroused overwhelming opposition among both laymen and clerics by his efforts to centralize authority and to transform Argentina's primitive economy and creole-Spanish culture with foreign aid. His foreign policy, too, gave offense to many Argentines: to some because of his coolness toward the current inter-American defense movement under Bolívar's leadership, and to many more because he failed to press vigorously Argentina's war with Brazil over Uruguay. The Constitution of 1826 was paralyzed from the start by the refusal of several provinces to ratify it. The spirit of revolt flared again and Facundo Quiroga egged the rebels on with the cry "Religion or death." In July 1827 Rivadavia resigned and left the country. Eighteen years later he died in Cadiz. Like San Martín, he passed his last years in virtual exile. Also like San Martín he has been placed on a pedestal

* Creole: native American of European stock.

by posterity, with the difference that extreme nationalists and right-wing Catholics have not yet absolved Rivadavia.

JUAN MANUEL DE ROSAS

Out of the confusion and violence following Rivadavia's fall emerged the latter's antithesis and Argentina's strong man from 1829 to 1852, Juan Manuel de Rosas. Called "The Restorer" (*El Restaurador*), Rosas earned his title in two ways. Although his administration soon evolved into a tyranny under the prodding of his ruthless helpmeet, Doña Encarnación, it arrested the disintegration of Argentina and restored a substantial measure of order and security for conformists. It also represented a creole, nativist reaction against Rivadavia's program of Europeanizing and modernizing Argentina.

The Force of Myth

Rosas was well prepared for his role. Although he came of an upper-class Buenos Aires family, he never travelled abroad until he was ousted in 1852. All his roots lay in Argentina and he was equally at home in the city and on the pampa. Much of his early life was spent among the gauchos, whom he could outride, outfight, and harangue in their own dialect. Yet he played with equal facility the role of *gran señor* and prided himself on the correctness of his Castilian grammar and the richness of his Castilian vocabulary. "Order and discipline" was his motto, which he enforced with qualities of leadership developed in an early life of almost constant conflict, now with other caudillos, now with the neighboring Indians of the pampa.

Born in 1793, Rosas first achieved national prominence through his election in 1829 as governor of the Province of Buenos Aires. After a two-year interval, he was re-elected in 1835 and thenceforth held the post uninterruptedly until his overthrow seventeen years later. Nominally, his rule never extended beyond his own province, except that by general agreement he was given control of Argentina's foreign relations. But this was an important exception, and thanks both to the advantage given him by the commercial and political pre-eminence of Buenos Aires, and to the fortuitous elimination of other provincial caudillos who might have been serious rivals, Rosas soon made himself master of all Argentina, the caudillo of all its caudillos. Although he exploited to the fullest the widespread Federalist hatred of the "dirty, traitorous Unitarians," he denied that he was a Federalist and in fact his principal service to his country, besides arresting its disintegration, was, however unintentionally, to lay the groundwork for its unification along Unitarian lines after his fall.

In foreign and ecclesiastical affairs, however, there was a sharp contrast between the policies of Rosas and those of the Unitarians. His foreign policy exhibited two of the most offensive traits of nationalism: xenophobia and aggressiveness. The leading example is his constant intervention in Uruguay, culminating in a ten-year siege of Montevideo. As a result, under his rule Argentina was almost constantly embroiled with foreign powers, including at various times France and Great Britain as well as neighboring Brazil. These three were partly responsible, for all of them likewise constantly meddled in River Plate affairs and in 1830 Britain seized the Falkland Islands in the Atlantic, which Argentina claimed. Yet Rosas clearly courted these foreign broils, though he sought to keep them short of war and continued to do business privately with the enemy. As the U.S. chargé in Buenos Aires, William Harris, wrote in 1849, Rosas wanted "not war exactly—but . . . something approaching it as nearly as possible, without the rigor and inconvenience of actual blows." Obviously, his purpose was to strengthen himself politically by appealing to national pride, and in this he succeeded for many years. Ultimately, however, his foreign policy led to his overthrow.

In contrast to the Unitarians, Rosas was a champion of the Catholic Church, though he asserted as strongly as any Unitarian the government's right to control appointment to ecclesiastical office and no more brooked opposition from clergymen than from laymen. The church was expected to reciprocate his protection of it by supporting him, as it did in a number of ways, most notably by permitting portraits of Rosas the Restorer to be placed on altars alongside statues of Christ the Redeemer.

Indeed, as one of his recent apologists has said, Rosas "erected the [Argentine] Federation into a religious faith and made himself its pontiff. . . . [He] divined the force of myth and decided to use it in defense of the unity of the fatherland [la patria]." That unity was to be complete: "one faith, one language, one ceremonial, one style," and it was to be inculcated by the schools and enforced not only by the government but also by a terrorist organization, the Mazorca. Yet, like many another Latin American dictator, Rosas gave lip service to liberty; to this end he sought to identify his regime with the May Doctrine and the independence movement. "The cause of the Federation," he declared in 1835, "is as national as that of independence."

Young Argentina

As the leader of a nationalistic reaction against the Unitarians' "exotic ideas," Rosas won for a short time the sympathy of the rising "Generation of 1837," a label applied to a group of young intellectuals, including Esteban Echeverría and Juan Bautista Alberdi, who belonged to the first generation brought up under the republic. These young men were strongly influenced by the European Romantic movement, political as well as literary, to which they were introduced by Echeverría on his return in 1830 from five years' residence in France. Politically, they responded most warmly to its romantic nationalism as represented by the German Johann Gottfried von Herder, whom they read in French translation. Following Herder, they concluded that Argentina must work out its national destiny within the terms prescribed by race and soil and revealed by history. This was the theme of an important paper read by Alberdi in July 1837 at the first meeting of the Literary Salon which some of them had just formed; in it, Alberdi spoke slightingly of Rivadavia as doctrinaire, while calling Rosas not only "great and powerful" but also "eminently representative," as evidenced by his popularity, "the most undeniable sign of the legitimacy of governments."

The Literary Salon's brief honeymoon with Rosas came to an end in 1838 when he broke with France, the source of the Salon's inspiration, and began his brutal repression of all dissent. An early victim was the Salon itself, which then went underground. Significantly, it took the new name "May Association" (Asociación de Mayo), indicating that what was at issue was not a particular regime or set of measures but the shaping of Argentina's future by the meaning given its basic ideals as expressed in the May Doctrine.

It soon turned out that the Generation of 1837 did in fact have much in common with Rivadavia. They, too, borrowed "exotic ideas": the first notable expression of their views, Echeverría's *Socialist Dogma*, applied to Argentine problems the ideas of European reformers, especially those of French pre-Marxist socialists. Also, for all their theoretical nativism, they sought, as Rivadavia had done, to transform Argentine culture by purging it of its "backward" Spanish elements and modernizing it on models provided by Europe and the United States. (There was an obvious dichotomy in their views; it still exists, and it has been a never-ending source of tension in Argentine public life.) Where they differed most from Rivadavia was in timing and temperament: they were not in so great a hurry, and they were less averse to concession and compromise. These proved to be decisive differences when Rosas was at last ousted.

Rosas' overthrow was brought about by a combination of many factors. One was the literary warfare waged against him by the intellectual exiles, including members of the May Association and others, such as Echeverría, Alberdi, Bartolomé Mitre, and Sarmiento. Most of them fled as the tyranny tightened from 1838 to 1840. Some took refuge in Montevideo, others in Bolivia, and still others in the greater security of Santiago, Chile, on the other side of the Andes. It was in Santiago that Sarmiento wrote his classic *Facundo* (1845), a book which took its title from the name of the caudillo, Facundo Quiroga, though it was aimed against Rosas. The book analyzed Argentina's troubles since independence in terms of a conflict between civilization, as represented by the cities, and barbarism, as represented by the caudillos and their supporting gaucho hordes. Its thesis has long been under fire, but it remains unrivalled as a picture of Argentine society in the age of Rosas.

These intellectual exiles provided most of Argentina's leadership in the generation after Rosas' fall, but the forces that ousted him were made up mainly of former provincial supporters who turned against him in the end, and foreign enemies. Chief among the former was Justo José Urquiza, wealthy caudillo of Entre Ríos, who resented Rosas' economic discrimination in favor of Buenos Aires over the other provinces and professed resentment also against his failure to establish constitutional government as promised from the start. The foreign enemies, provoked by Rosas' long intervention in Uruguay, were the Empire of Brazil and an Uruguayan faction.

Urquiza raised the standard of revolt in 1851 and was joined by forces from the other two countries. When the allied army met Rosas' troops at Monte Caseros early the following year, most of the latter deserted and the small remnant was soon beaten. No one rallied to Rosas' defense; a sympathetic historian admits that the people at large were tired of him and ready for a change. Rosas, with his daughter, took refuge on a British ship at Buenos Aires, sailed to England and remained there in obscure retirement until his death at Southampton a quarter century later.

Transition: Foundations of Modern Argentina, 1853-1880

The fall of Rosas was final and complete. He never returned, and unlike Perón a century later, he retained no organized following in Argentina. His influence there survived mainly in the nostalgic literature of the romanticized gaucho, of which the first notable example was the poem *Martín Fierro* (1872). Equally decisive, and almost equally quick, was the victory of Rosas' enemies, in the sense that within a year they had given Argentina the liberal constitution under which it is still governed and had started it on the liberal economic policy that ultimately transformed an aggregation of backward provinces into the leading nation of Latin America.

The abruptness of the change was more apparent than real; in its political aspect it was not fully accomplished until 1880. The intervening period of more than a quarter century (longer than the period covered by Rosas' rule) was one of transition from the old regime to the new. Although the supreme caudillo was gone, powerful provincial caudillos remained; it took more than two decades of almost constant fighting to reduce the last of them. There also remained the knotty problem of the relationship of Buenos Aires to the rest of the country, which had contributed to Rosas' undoing and which continued to occasion civil strife until 1880. Moreover, the colonial traits, both economic and social, that had continued to mark Argentine society strongly in the time of Rosas were slow to change after his fall. As late as 1869, according to its first national census, Argentina still had a population of only 1,830,224, which represented an increase of only 3 to 1 in the last 70 years (in the same period, the population of the United States had increased sevenfold). In racial composition, too, the late colonial pattern still remained substantially unchanged in 1869: three fourths Indian and mestizo, less than one fifth white, and the rest Negro and mulatto. Railway mileage, which was to pass the 20,000 mark by 1913, still remained under 1,500 as late as 1880. In the next generation Argentina was to change with dizzying rapidity in all these respects, and others as well.

Yet the groundwork for this revolution was laid during the transitional period from 1853 to 1880. The main problems were to attract foreign capital investments and immigrants, to employ modern technology, to clear away Indian obstructions, and to create a favorable political climate by establishing a reasonable degree of order and security. Collateral problems arising out of Argentina's relations with her neighbors threatened at times to overshadow the rest; chief among the former was the Paraguayan War of 1865-1870.

The Constitution of 1853: Disunion and Reunion

The new regime was almost wrecked at the start by the refusal of Buenos Aires province to join the union established by the other provinces under a constitution drawn up by a convention at Santa Fe in 1853. Its framers were animated by the spirit of conciliation expressed in General Urquiza's motto after the fall and flight of Rosas: "Neither victors nor vanquished" (*Ni vencedores ni vencidos*). Seeking to reconcile Federals and Unitarians, they produced a constitution modelled on that of the United States in most respects. It provided for a federal system of representative government based on a division of power between the central government and the provinces, and on the separation of powers, executive, legislative, and judicial. These were vested respectively in a president, a bicameral Congress (Senate and Chamber of Deputies), and a hierarchy of federal courts headed by a Supreme Court, with the three powers interconnected by a system of checks and balances. In fact, the resemblance to the North American model was so close that for many years Argentine courts interpreted their country's constitution in the light of interpretations of the constitution of the United States by its courts and leading commentators.

Some departures from the model were made, however, in order to

meet Argentina's particular needs, as Juan Bautista Alberdi had coun-
selled in a work, commonly referred to as *Bases*,* written specially
for the occasion. The departures included a six-year term for the
president, and no immediate re-election, and the provision for state
support of the Roman Catholic Church, coupled with a guarantee of
freedom of conscience and public worship for other religious faiths.
A major difference soon developed in practice under the article
authorizing federal intervention in the provinces. A somewhat similar
provision in the constitution of the United States has remained
largely a dead letter, but in Argentina such interventions were numerous from the start; by 1943 they numbered 142, and they had
long since converted the nominally federal system into one of a
highly centralized, unitary character.

Despite the refusal of the province of Buenos Aires to ratify it, the
constitution was proclaimed on July 9, 1853, the anniversary of
Argentina's declaration of independence. Urquiza was elected president for the term 1853-1859.

One of several features of the constitution that made it unaccept-
able to the province of Buenos Aires was the stipulation that the city
of Buenos Aires should be the capital of the republic. The province
was determined not to be bereft of its chief city, and both province
and city were likewise determined not to let the central government
take over the customs revenues of the port, which were the largest
source of revenue in all Argentina. In their eyes, Urquiza's election
as president compounded the offense, for most *porteños*,† former
Federals and Unitarians alike, were unwilling to join a union headed
by a man from another province, especially when that man was
Urquiza. Their deep hostility to him rested on various grounds—
because he was a *caudillo* (Sarmiento never forgave him for this),
or because he had supported the tyranny of Rosas for so many years,
or because of his alleged subservience to Brazil, which continued to
intervene in Uruguay and in the Plata area at large, with little or no
objection from Urquiza. And finally, there was a personal factor:
young Bartolomé Mitre of Buenos Aires was emerging as a rival to the
old caudillo of Entre Ríos for national leadership.

---

* Full title: *Bases y puntos de partida para la organización política de la república argentina.*
† Residents of the port city *par excellence*, Buenos Aires.

Such considerations of interest and pride, local and personal, had more to do with keeping Buenos Aires out of the union for the rest of the decade than did disagreement over the main provisions of the constitution. Urquiza's stand on the controversial question of modernization and economic development with foreign aid had nothing to do with it, for he followed the same policy in this respect as that advocated by his severest critics in Buenos Aires, such as Sarmiento and Mitre. Economic liberalism was in fact written into the constitution, which favored foreign investments. The alacrity with which Urquiza adopted this policy was surprising in a man who was a provincial magnate of the old school, a kind of backwoods baron, whose great wealth consisted mainly in land and cattle and whose power was built up with the aid of his gaucho hordes. Alberdi's influence may have aided in his conversion. At any rate, Urquiza was converted and Alberdi broke with his own Buenos Aires friends to serve him through a diplomatic mission to Europe. Urquiza contracted with William Wheelwright, an American citizen, to build a railroad from Rosario to Córdoba; with a Swiss entrepreneur to build the Argentine section of a projected trans-Andean railroad to Chile; and with Frenchmen and other foreigners for such undertakings as the promotion of immigration, the exploration of the Chaco, and the preparation of an atlas of Argentina. The caudillo even turned Maecenas, employing the Italian-trained Uruguayan painter, Juan Manuel Blanes, to decorate the private chapel on his estate in Entre Ríos.

Tension mounted between Buenos Aires and the rest of the country as the metropolis prospered under a free trade policy that exposed formerly protected domestic industries in the other provinces to disastrous foreign competition. Both sides started playing for keeps: the Confederation undertook to build up its principal port, Rosario, as a rival to Buenos Aires; the latter moved to make its secession permanent by obtaining foreign recognition of its independence; and each side sought to weaken the other by subversion and even assassination.

That civil war resulted is much less surprising than the form it took. It consisted of only two battles separated by two years of relatively peaceful coexistence. At Cepeda in 1859 Urquiza's Confederation forces defeated those of Buenos Aires under Mitre. Thereupon, Buenos Aires agreed to enter the union on the basis of certain constitutional amendments; and, Urquiza's term having expired, he was succeeded in the presidency by one Santiago Derqui, who was supposed to appease the interprovincial conflict by governing in the interest of the republic at large. But the conflict was not appeased: in 1861 Buenos Aires, still led by Mitre, appealed to arms. Again a single battle was fought. This time, at Pavón, Mitre won; although the battle was a draw, Urquiza for some reason retired with his troops to Entre Ríos, leaving Buenos Aires in control not only of the battlefield but also, as it turned out, of the whole Argentine political arena.

Compared with the civil wars of the same period in Mexico (1857-1860) and the United States (1861-1865), this Argentine conflict was a tame affair, and when there was fighting it had something of the stylized, ritual character of a combat between champions in Trojan or medieval times. It was not that the Argentines of that age were tame or squeamish about bloodletting. On the contrary, the gauchos were notoriously quick and deadly with the knife, and the opposing forces of civilization were not far behind them in ferocity: Sarmiento once urged General Mitre "not to be economical with the blood of gauchos," whom he described as fit only to fertilize the soil of Argentina with their carcasses. Rather, the moderation of this two-year conflict bespoke widespread agreement among the leading contestants on two fundamental issues: the unity of Argentina, and its modernization. Urquiza played a decisive role as pacificator in this situation. He may have yielded at Pavón in order to avert a mutually destructive civil war; certainly from that time forth, until his assassination in 1870 during an uprising in his home province, he gave powerful support to the *porteño*-dominated regime against the provincial caudillos and other disruptive elements that continued to harass it. In so doing, he represented those strong forces outside of Buenos Aires that were working for national unity and modernization and without whose support the new Argentina could never have been fashioned.

The Argentine Republic's First Three Presidents

For a dozen years after Pavón, Buenos Aires dominated Argentina through two dynamic presidents. The first was its native son Mitre, from 1862 to 1868. The second, for the next six years, was Domingo Sarmiento, who, though a native of far western San Juan, had identified himself with Buenos Aires since his return from exile following Rosas' fall. Significantly, under the constitutional amendments of 1860, and beginning with Mitre's administration, the terms "Argentine Republic" and "Argentine nation" first came into regular official use. During Urquiza's administration, the designation had been Argentine Confederation, and prior to that, United Provinces of the Río de la Plata; both terms were retained in the compromise of 1853 for old times' sake, but they fell into disuse. The national aspiration was now widespread, and it was fortified by Mitre and Sarmiento with the aid of the extensive powers conferred on the president by the constitution and sanctioned by a society that respects leadership.

Mitre and Sarmiento had many things in common besides their service in the presidency and their devotion to the policy of modernizing Argentina. Both saw military service, both were journalists, both wrote books about Argentina that became classics, and both contributed in these and other ways to establishing what has been called the "canonical nationalism" of Argentina on the basis of the May Doctrine.

At the same time, the two men differed sharply in other respects. Unlike Sarmiento, Mitre did not merely write for newspapers, but founded one, La Nación (1870), which became a kind of national institution. In their books, Mitre was the conventional historian (though of a scholarly type new to Argentina) and wrote about national heroes, San Martín and Belgrano, whereas Sarmiento was by turns polemicist, prose poet, and philosopher, and wrote about national villains, the caudillos and their gauchos. Mitre gave the impression of picturing himself alternately as a representative of one or another European type, sometimes as a romantic freedom fighter like the Italian patriot Garibaldi, who had aided the Argentine exiles in their struggle against Rosas, and at other times as an Argentine counterpart of the frock-coated French statesman-historian Guizot. Sarmiento, on the other hand, was the New World incarnate. In spite of himself, he had much of the gaucho in his make-up; in later life his model was the United States, which he visited in 1847 as a tourist and in 1865-1868 as Argentina's minister plenipotentiary, and which he admired so greatly that he urged his fellow countrymen to "North Americanize" Argentina.

While there were likewise differences as well as resemblances between the presidential administrations of Mitre and Sarmiento, the basic similarities predominate so strongly that, on the scale on which they have to be viewed here, the two administrations merge to form one continuous whole. On the constructive side, both sought to accelerate the modernization of Argentina through foreign investment and immigration, modern technology, and education. They met with substantial success. Under Mitre, some 800 miles of railway was constructed with the aid of British capital, equipment, and technical skill. Under Sarmiento, some 280,000 immigrants entered the country, despite epidemics of cholera (1870) and yellow fever (1871), and the volume of foreign commerce increased by 70 per cent. Together, they gave Argentina the best public school system in Latin America, and Sarmiento—a friend of Horace Mann, pioneer of public education in the United States—founded a teachers' training school with personnel brought from the United States. Also, both administrations, forced to cope with frequent attacks by Indians and caudillos, imported modern weapons, such as Remington rifles, which ultimately provided the margin of victory.

Finally, continuity was given their administrations by the Paraguayan War, which began in 1865 under Mitre and ended in 1870 under Sarmiento. Argentina, allied with Uruguay and Brazil, proclaimed it to the Paraguayans as a war for their liberation from the dictator of Paraguay. The Paraguayans, however, resisted such liberation until four fifths of their male population had been wiped out. That it took the allies so long to win is explained partly by the fact that Paraguay, although the smallest country in South America, had the largest army in South America as well as the advantages of a defensive position and interior lines; it is also explained by the inherent weakness of all coalitions.

For Argentina the Paraguayan War was costly and unrewarding. The territorial gains went mainly to Brazil, partly under an arbitral award made years later by the President of the United States; and Brazil's preponderant position in the Plata basin was further fortified. As Argentines look back, the only feature of the war that they view with satisfaction is the phrase struck off by their foreign minister at its close: "Victory gives no rights" (La victoria no da derechos). Even this is applauded through a common misunderstanding: it was not, as generally believed, a high-minded self-denying ordinance, but a caveat against apprehended encroachments on Paraguay by Argentina's stronger ally, Brazil. Argentina has never fought another foreign war.

Mitre and Sarmiento differed on one aspect of foreign policy. While Mitre described his policy as "American and good-neighborly," he was opposed to involving Argentina in multilateral security arrangements such as those planned by a conference of Spanish American states at Lima in 1865. Sarmiento took the opposite view, but nothing came of his advocacy of multilateral cooperation, for the Lima conference proved to be the last of a series of Latin American essays at reciprocal defense reaching back to Bolívar's Panama Congress of 1826. By the time the new Pan American movement was launched in 1889, Sarmiento was dead.

At the end of Sarmiento's term, provincial opposition to the continuance of *porteño* domination helped to bring about the election to the presidency of a native of the northern province of Tucumán, talented young Nicolás Avellaneda (1874-1880), who had been Sarmiento's Minister of Public Instruction. Intransigent Buenos Aires, alleging corruption and led by Mitre, revolted; but the revolt was soon put down, with few lives lost and no proscriptions afterwards. The change to a president from the interior made little difference; in fact, Avellaneda had already moved to Buenos Aires and served in its provincial government before entering Sarmiento's cabinet. He continued his two predecessors' policy of modernization with foreign aid and met with some success despite the panic-depression of 1873-1878 that afflicted Argentina in common with the United States and other countries of the Atlantic world. In one respect, the depression was beneficial to Argentina, for by sharply reducing imports it stimulated the local manufacture of consumer goods, such as newsprint and furniture, and the processing of foodstuffs.

The main feature of Avellaneda's administration, however, was the "Conquest of the Desert," which was begun and largely accomplished in 1879 by General Julio A. Roca. Except for minor mopping-up operations that continued for several years, this completed the centuries-long cycle of Argentina's Indian wars, so that Roca has been called the last of the *conquistadores*. As in the United States about the same time, the Indians were either killed off or bottled up in reservations. Despite its name, the territories opened up by this conquest were not a desert but included rich pampa lands as well as bleak but valuable stretches of Patagonia. Argentina's hold on the latter was thus secured against the threat of Chilean encroachment, and the way was cleared for the great surge forward into the pampas which was a main source of Argentina's unparalleled prosperity in the next third of a century. And *conquistador* Roca was started on the steep but short road that led him a year later to the presidency.

THREE

TRANSFORMING A NATION:

MODERNIZATION AND THE IMMIGRANT FLOOD

1880-1916

For a third of a century after 1880 the policies described at the end of the preceding chapter were applied with great success by a new oligarchy. Argentina grew prodigiously in population, wealth, and other respects, and assumed its modern aspect. Almost all its present railway network, still the largest in Latin America and seventh largest in the world, was built during this period. Its colonial economy was transformed through the spread of commercialized agriculture, and by the end of the period it was one of the world's largest exporters of cereals and meat. Its ethnic composition was revolutionized by a sustained flood of immigration, mainly from Italy and Spain. Total population shot up from an estimated 2,600,-000 in 1880 to census figures of 3,955,000 in 1895 and 7,885,000 in 1914, and in the latter year the proportion of foreign-born reached the extraordinarily high figure of 30 per cent.

Yet contrary to the current experience of many underdeveloped countries, which are finding that population growth frustrates aspirations for a more abundant life, Argentina's per capita wealth grew five times as fast as its rapidly expanding population between 1886 and 1914. Likewise, the literacy rate rose steeply, from 22 per cent in 1869 to 46 per cent in 1895 and 65 per cent in 1914. Rebuilt in the 1880s for beauty as well as business, Buenos Aires had become one of the great cultural centers of Latin America by the end of this period. There was political progress as well: A long, hard struggle against the entrenched oligarchy culminated in 1916 in the victory

41

of a party of protest, the Radical Civic Union, and the election of Argentina's first president who was a man of the people, Hipólito Irigoyen. In today's perspective the event appears less crucial than it once did, but is still significant enough to serve as the terminal point for the present chapter.

Today, there are Argentines as well as Frenchmen who regard the years just before the World War of 1914 as their country's *belle époque*. At the time, however, many people in Argentina did not find the epoch at all beautiful. Among these were creoles of the old school who had a fancied *belle époque* of their own—the period before fearless gauchos, easy-going small towns, and immemorial native customs were overwhelmed by modernization and hordes of immigrants with their strange, hard-working ways. The immigrants themselves were unhappy over being treated as second-class citizens, and there were Argentines who wanted modernization and progress but were shocked by the shoddy ways in which these were being achieved.

In addition, this material progress created or sharpened resentments that were to agitate the nation for decades to come. It stimulated the growth of both the middle class and the proletariat, and both felt defrauded of social justice and rightful participation in public affairs. It produced a one-sided, vulnerable economy, overspecialized in commercial agriculture and too dependent on foreign markets, manufactures, and capital. Finally, it gave British and other foreign investors and businessmen control of key sectors of the Argentine economy and at the same time identified them in the public mind as parties to a "corrupt alliance" with Argentina's new and increasingly unpopular oligarchy.

The New Oligarchy, 1880-1912

The new oligarchy that was to rule Argentina for a third of a century owed its origin and character largely to the outcome of the wars, Indian and civil, of 1879-80, described at the end of the preceding chapter. Their combined effect was greatly to reduce the American and enhance the European factor in Argentine life, and to produce both a new scale of values, dominated by dedication to material progress, and also a new national leadership representing the pacification finally achieved between Buenos Aires and the provinces.

There was no abrupt break with the past in 1880. On the contrary, the preceding regime, too, had been a *de facto* oligarchy or, to put it another way, a limited democracy ruled by an elite of large landowners. Also, the new oligarchy's program of economic development was substantially identical with the one advocated since the 1850s by Alberdi, Mitre, and Sarmiento. The difference was one of degree and emphasis rather than of kind. Yet the difference soon became so great that before the new oligarchy's first decade was out, the older leaders were charging it with betraying the ideals of 1853 by its materialism, selfishness, and corruption.

At its best, the new oligarchy was represented by Julio A. Roca and Carlos Pellegrini, who formed a team during a large part of this era, though they had a falling out toward its close. Roca, born at Tucumán in 1843 of an old creole family, represented the provinces. He was also a professional soldier, but not the bluff, plainspoken type: his nickname was "The Fox" (*el Zorro*). Pellegrini represented the new Buenos Aires. He was a principal founder, in 1881, of one of the boom city's most symbolic institutions, the luxurious Jockey Club, citadel of the *porteño* upper class for decades to come. Yet he was appropriately known as "The Gringo," for both his parents were immigrants: his father, a French–Italian engineer from Savoy; his mother, English and a sister of the noted statesman, orator, and free-trader, John Bright; and he made no bones about his admiration for England, France, and the United States, all of which he visited time and again. He was tall, Roca short; both men had blue eyes and a fair complexion, as no Argentine writer seems to have failed to note; and both men were not only presidents of Argentina but shaped the country's destiny in other ways as well.

Roca was president twice, the first time from 1880 to 1886. From the start he gave a new tone to public affairs by taking as his motto "Peace and administration," which, as applied, meant adjourning disputes about theory and principle and getting on with the pursuit of happiness and wealth, especially through the exploitation of the resources opened up by Roca's own recent conquest of the desert. The boom that resulted will be described later, but here it should be noted that Roca and his successor pushed through Argentina's first anticlerical legislation. This included laws requiring civil marriage ceremonies (though not interfering with religious ceremonies) and prohibiting religious instruction in public schools during regular school hours. As Argentine Catholic spokesmen such as José Manuel Estrada complained, this new legislation violated the spirit of the church-state settlement achieved by the founding fathers in 1853-1860. And yet it was in harmony with the completely secularized outlook of the new oligarchy and its gospel of wealth.

This gospel became a caricature under Roca's successor and kinsman of Córdoba, Miguel Juárez Celman. Policy did not change, but administration did. Following the government's own example set in its ill-timed stimulation of railway investments, the country became involved in an orgy of speculation. At the same time, price inflation reduced real wages, and the workers had no effective remedy in labor unions, which were just beginning to take shape. As a result, while the boom lasted, the rich got richer and the poor got poorer, and when the financial crash came it soon brought the administration tumbling down in the so-called Revolution of 1890, which was in fact only an unsuccessful revolt.

Actually, the revolt changed little beyond forcing the President's resignation, and one of the main reasons why it merits notice here is that it exhibits the tenacity and adaptability of the new oligarchs at this stage. Pellegrini and Roca, vice president and minister of war respectively under Juárez Celman, first suppressed the revolt and then forced the discredited president to resign. Pellegrini replaced him and filled out the term, to 1892. By a succession of personal and institutional changes and political maneuvers, he and Roca determined the course of public policy during most of the next two decades. This involved not only the continuation of the oligarchy in power. It also involved a return to the sound development policy of earlier years and the maintenance of good relations with European centers of capital investment, thus paving the way for Argentina's greatest leap forward, which took place in the first decade of the twentieth century.

Those who like to speculate about the might-have-beens of history will find the crisis of 1890 exceptionally rich in food for thought. The policy preferred by Juárez Celman was one of "repudiation and further inflation." Such a course was followed by other Latin American governments, including Venezuela, both before and after 1890. Had Argentina embarked on it in that year, its whole future would probably have been quite different, and more like that of the bankrupt Venezuela of 1902, in which Britain and Germany intervened by force of arms (as some Britons urged their government to do in Argentina in 1890).

The Revolution of 1890 also deserves note as marking an epoch in the growth of organized political opposition in Argentina. One of the preliminaries of the outbreak was the creation in 1889 of the Civic Union (Unión Cívica), a loose combination of malcontents of various kinds. These included a youth movement; reformers among the older oligarchy, led by Mitre; Leandro Alem and his numerous following among the middle class and the workers; and a substantial group of army officers, one of whom, young José E. Uriburu, was to be heard from again in later years. After the suppression of the revolt, the unwieldy Civic Union split. The larger group, led by Alem, tacked "Radical" on to the original name, formally organizing in 1892 as the Radical Civil Union. Commonly called the Radicals or U.C.R., this party followed a frankly revolutionary course for the next two decades. The more conservative wing of the Civic Union, led by Mitre, continued to call for reform but not revolution. Both wings were frustrated by the new oligarchy, whose political instrument, the National Autonomous Party, remained in power until 1916.

Until the adoption of the epochal Saenz Peña Law in 1912,* the conservatives kept a firm hold on power in the face of a double threat: from the rising Radical party, which lived up to its motto of "abstention and revolution," and from a terrorist campaign conducted by anarchists, most of whom were Italian, Spanish, and Russian immigrants. As early as 1902, in an effort to stamp out anarchism, a Law of Residence was enacted which authorized the summary deportation of foreign revolutionaries. Despite rigorous enforcement of the law, violence continued to mount. In 1910 it provoked the imposition of a state of siege, and in 1912, after a visit to Argentina, James Bryce noted "the emergence here and nowhere else in South America of a vehement anarchist propaganda." However unintentionally, the anarchists' activities may have contributed to the Radicals' victory by helping to convince the conservatives that even reform is preferable to revolution.

* The name is usually written Sáenz, but the accent was omitted by the author of this law.

Support by the military may be part of the answer to the question of how the conservatives clung to power so long, but they were also aided by divisions among their more numerous enemies. The Radicals had no national organization in most of the provinces until 1910, lagged behind their Socialist rivals in the all-important city of Buenos Aires, and suffered from leadership problems. Their first head, Alem, committed suicide in 1896, and his successor and nephew, Hipólito Irigoyen,* who was to emerge finally as a messiah, looked for several years more like a power-hungry muddler. At an early date he alienated two of the party's best men, Juan B. Justo and Lisandro de la Torre, who founded rival parties, the Socialist and the Progressive Democratic respectively; and his only serious attempt at revolution, in 1905, was badly botched. As for the Socialists, their strength was confined almost exclusively to Buenos Aires. Their leader, Justo, was a physician turned intellectual, and there was little revolutionary appeal in their program, which was so moderate and gradual that today they would be grouped with the Democratic Left rather than the Marxists.

Nor should it be forgotten that these were prosperous years for Argentina, especially for the key city of Buenos Aires. A good deal of this prosperity trickled down. James Bryce reported that: ". . . Though no doubt there is an ostentatious display of wealth [in Argentina], work is more abundant and wages are higher than in any other part of the world."

Prosperity and rising living standards can generate political revolutions in the long run, but their short-range effect is often to pacify discontents. So it was in the Argentina of these years, and the oligarchs' ultimate loss of power was due to their own inner divisions and to the concessions they made—under pressure, to be sure, but peaceably—which could be styled a species of political suicide.

The conservative split began in 1901 with a definitive personal rupture between Roca, now in his second term as president, and Pellegrini. The occasion was a debt consolidation agreement negotiated by Pellegrini with Argentina's European creditors. At first Roca approved the agreement, but when a formidable explosion of injured national pride was generated by a clause giving the foreign creditors a measure of control over Argentina's customs revenues, the Fox

* Also written Yrigoyen.

beat a hasty retreat and left the Gringo to take all the blame. Pellegrini not only never forgave Roca, but also, from that time forth, became more and more critical of the oligarchy's imposition of limited democracy by force and fraud—a system he had formerly endorsed and exploited. The time had come, Pellegrini now said, to change all this and open the floodgates to democracy.

This was Pellegrini's plea in his last speech in Congress, June 11, 1906. Discussing an amnesty bill in favor of those implicated in the latest revolt, that of 1905, he recalled that this would be the fifth amnesty in the last few years as the nation repeated with "dolorous regularity" its too familiar round of rebellion, repression, and pardon. Then, after telling how his hopes of a solution through evolution rather than revolution had been disappointed, he concluded that there would never be peace and union in "the Argentine family" until all Argentines enjoyed equal rights and were no longer faced with the alternative of either renouncing their status as citizens or taking up arms to recover their rights.

Transition

Pellegrini died in 1906, as did Mitre. A new generation was taking over in Argentina. One of its best representatives, though by no means its youngest, was Roque Saenz Peña, a scion of the old oligarchy but a philosophical liberal. He had first won a measure of fame by his Byronic gesture of fighting on Peru's side against Chile in the War of the Pacific (1879-1883), and in 1890, at the first Pan American Conference, he made a widely acclaimed speech against Secretary of State Blaine's plea for an American customs union, opposing Blaine's motto "America for the Americans" with his own device, "America for humanity." A few years later liberals gave him strong support for the presidency, but he was maneuvered into withdrawing by the nomination of his conservative father. In 1910, however, he was elected president without opposition. With the Radicals still abstaining and the other parties in a state of flux, he was in effect a nonpartisan candidate and so regarded himself. No one knew exactly what to expect from him, but liberals liked him for his record, conservatives for his standing in the social register.

Another event of 1910 was the centennial celebration of Argentina's May Revolution and independence. It took place during a kind of brief era of good feelings among Argentines, for the Radicals were momentarily quiescent and only the anarchists (foreigners, of course) continued to disturb the peace. Carlos Ibarguren, an eyewitness, comments on the celebration thus:

> Those of us who felt the patriotic vibration that moved our souls in those unforgettable days and were present at the magnificent homage paid Argentina by all the nations of the world by sending to Buenos Aires illustrious statesmen and ambassadors, royalty such as the Infanta Isabel of Spain and chiefs of state such as President Montt of Chile, found proof in this great ceremony, in which civilized humanity celebrated the first century of our independent political life, of the realization of the happy augury in the verse of our national anthem: "A new and glorious nation arises . . . and the free men of the world respond, 'To the great Argentine people, hail.' "

In the event, many conservatives came to regard Saenz Peña as a traitor to his class. Making full use of the extensive powers of his office, he pushed through a reluctant conservative Congress the Electoral Laws of 1912 (commonly called collectively the Saenz Peña Law), which virtually assured a Radical victory at the next election. Radical historians like to give the credit for it to Irigoyen, and he may deserve some of it, but it was the kind of reform that Saenz Peña, along with Pellegrini and other "liberal Tories," had been urging for years: a reform that would make democracy effective. Another important purpose was to promote the two-party system, as the best warranty that effective democracy would produce responsible government. To these ends the law provided for: (1) the secret ballot, in place of the voice voting that had enabled landowners and employers to coerce their workers, tenants, and other dependents at the polls; (2) a new and honest registration of voters; (3) compulsory voting; and (4) the so-called "incomplete list," under which two thirds of the posts at stake in a constituency were allocated to the party with the largest vote, and the remaining third to the second largest.

Everything depended, of course, on honest administration of the law. Although Saenz Peña died in 1914, the vice president who succeeded him saw to it that it was administered honestly as far as his authority extended. As foreseen, the result was the election of the Radicals' presidential candidate, Hipólito Irigoyen. Yet it was a limited, personal victory. Though his majority in the popular vote was large, he won by the narrowest of margins in the Electoral College, and the conservatives still controlled Congress and 11 of the 14 provincial governments. The reform served one of its purposes brilliantly: the proportion of voters more than trebled, rising from 9 per cent of the adult male population in 1910 to 30 per cent in 1916. And under Argentine constitutional law and practice the powers of the president are so great that, once in office, Irigoyen could be expected to extend and strengthen the Radicals' control of the national and provincial governments—as he did with a vengeance in the course of his six-year term. But the oligarchy was by no means done for. Some of its members had joined the rather amorphous Radical party and came to power with it.

Economic Explosion

The conquest of the desert in 1879 and the settlement of the Buenos Aires question in 1880 triggered three decades of economic expansion which at times became so rapid that it seemed more like an explosion. It took place under a system of modified laissez-faire, with the government stepping in occasionally to help with subsidies or otherwise, but generally keeping hands off. It realized the dreams of Argentine leaders from Rivadavia and Alberdi to Roca and Pellegrini. But it could not have been accomplished if it had not also responded to European needs to import foodstuffs and export manufactures, capital, and emigrants. And, as it happened, the view prevailing in Argentina at this time was propitious to an accommodation between its own interests and those of Europe. Save for an occasional dissenter, Argentine opinion favored foreign investments, mainly from Britain, and foreign immigrants, mainly from Italy and Spain. Both investments and immigrants poured in on a grand scale in the 1880s and from the turn of the century to 1914; in between, both were reduced by the depression that triggered revolt in 1890 and continued almost to the end of that decade.

The most striking feature of Argentina's amazingly rapid economic development during this third of a century was the growth of its foreign component. In terms of production, the greatest increase was in commodities for the export market: cereals, meat, wool. In terms of national income, by 1914 more than 30 per cent of this was derived from foreign trade, as compared with about 10 per cent in the United States at that time. In terms of control of the economy, key sectors were in foreign hands, with the British in the forefront; they owned most of the railroads and grain elevators and many public utilities, shared ownership of the principal meat-packing plants (*frigoríficos*) with the United States, dominated banking, credit, and steamship lines, and furnished the chief market for Argentine products.

Already by 1890 the Anglo-American tie had become so important to Great Britain that the Argentine crisis of that year threatened to bankrupt not only the principal British creditor, Baring Brothers, but the Bank of England itself. The tie could not fail to mean even more to underdeveloped Argentina. Realization of the degree of her dependence on the British soon began to rankle. In 1896 Juan B. Justo said in a newspaper article:

> English capital has done what their armies could not do. Today our country is tributary to England. . . . No one can deny the benefits that the railroads, the gas plants, the streetcars, and the telegraph and telephone lines have brought us. . . . But the gold that the English capitalists take out of Argentina or carry off in the form of products, does us no more good than the Irish got from the revenues that the English lords took out of Ireland. . . . We also suffer from absentee capital. . . . It is this capital that largely prevents us from having sound money and obliges our financial market to submit to a continuous drain of hard currency.*

The greatest proportionate increase in British investments in Argentina took place in the 1880s, during which they grew from about $125 million to $850 million. By 1889 Argentina was absorbing between 40 and 50 per cent of all British foreign investments. The money went into government bonds, mortgages on lands, and various joint stock enterprises, but above all into railways. The crash of 1890 slowed British investment down for a decade, but with the return of prosperity after 1900 the pace accelerated again, and by 1910 the total amounted to nearly $1,500 million. By this time, however, British investors were beginning to play it safe along established lines and the initiative in providing risk capital was passing to the United

---

* José Luis Romero, *A History of Argentine Political Thought,* tr. and ed. by Thomas F. McGann (Stanford University Press, 1963), p. 193. By permission of Stanford University Press.

States, which had the advantage in supplying agricultural machinery and was entering the *frigorífico* field, and to Germany in commercial ventures. But on the whole, British primacy in Argentina was still unchallenged when World War I broke out in 1914.

Argentina's railroads were built mainly with British capital, which controlled 65 per cent of them by 1910. The rest were financed by French and Argentine government capital; Argentine private investors contributed little. Public subsidies, land grants, and guarantees of dividends often aided construction, but the trend was against government ownership and operation. In the crisis of 1890 the profitable *Oeste* line, owned by the province of Buenos Aires, was sold to private British interests.

Most of the railroads were built after 1879. The mileage increased from only 1,500 in that year to some 10,000 in 1900 and 18,000 in 1901. All the lines converged on Buenos Aires and they were confined very largely to the northern half of the country. There they served mainly the already settled area of the littoral and the newly opened pampa, although they also extended to Salta and Jujuy in the far northwest and beyond Mendoza to Chile, with which Argentina was linked by the Trans-Andine Railway.

Among the chief factors in Argentina's rapid growth during this period were low labor costs and an abundance of new, fertile land in the pampa area. The railroads made both of these possible by providing transportation in areas remote from navigable streams, and by facilitating settlement and attracting immigrants. Other factors were the introduction of alfalfa for feed and of barbed wire, which made cheap fencing possible for the first time in the treeless, stoneless pampa; the improvement of local breeds of cattle and sheep by crossing them with imported stock; the building of windmills to pump water; and the development of refrigeration both for packing plants and for trans-Atlantic ships. The first such ship, which sailed from Argentina to France in 1882, was French and appropriately bore the name *Frigorifique*, but England soon became, and has remained, much the largest purchaser of Argentina's chief meat products, beef and mutton. And in the background was the one big factor that made the growth of the Argentine economy feasible: the increasing European demand for the kind of foodstuffs Argentina was so well fitted to produce on a large scale.

The result was a tremendous expansion of Argentina's cultivated area, stockraising, and export trade in foodstuffs. The area under cultivation increased fourfold between 1872 and 1888. Frozen meat exports increased sixfold in the three years after 1885. Formerly an importer of wheat from as far away as the United States, Argentina began to export it in the 1870s on a small scale, which rapidly moved up to the substantial figure of 238,000 tons in 1887. By 1909 Argentina had become the world's largest exporter of grains. This economic revolution was first pastoral, then agricultural. In 1880, pastoral products made up 94 per cent of all Argentine exports, and agricultural products only 2 per cent, but by 1908 the roles had been reversed, and the figures were 30 per cent and 65 per cent respectively.

A similar growth had begun in the United States several decades earlier, and was still going on, but the results were substantially different from Argentina's in two respects. In the first place, population moved westward in the United States, whereas in Argentina after 1880 it was the grain-growing eastern provinces of the littoral that grew most rapidly. In the second place, farms of small or moderate size continued to predominate in the United States, but the old Argentine pattern of the *latifundio* or big estate was not only maintained but strengthened. The lack of an Argentine equivalent of the United States' Homestead Law of 1863 was only one reason for the difference; other reasons included a combination of Argentine circumstances, such as a chaotic land title system, traditions of personalism and graft, and an oligarchical regime, which facilitated the accumulation of large landholdings. Attempts at land reform had been made in the early years of independence but were undone by the tyrant Rosas, and the performance of the liberals who ousted him was no better than his in this respect.

What happened to the golden opportunity for land reform afforded by the conquest of the desert is typical. It opened up great stretches of desirable land to settlement, and veterans of the campaign were rewarded with land grants on a fairly equitable basis, in proportion to rank and service. These, however, averaged about 20,000 acres each, and the recipients had to go to so much trouble and expense in locating, surveying, and registering their claims that many of them were sold at a heavy discount and ended up in the hands of a few monopolists. In addition, it was at most times the general practice to sell public lands in large blocks; one authority describes a case in 1891 in which 88 holders thus acquired over five million hectares,* an average of some 147,000 acres per holder. It has also been pointed out that operation in large farm units is a consequence of the nature of Argentine agriculture, which is extensive, not intensive, and produces for export markets on a low-cost basis. Group colonization, with the land allocated in farms of moderate size, was attempted in Argentina many times from the 1850s on, and several of the efforts were successful, but their aggregate volume was not large enough to alter the general pattern of landholding.

For these and other reasons, large landholding continued to predominate. The census of 1914 showed that 78.3 per cent of all land in Argentina was held in farms of 2,500 acres or more; that there were some 4,400 properties of 12,000 to 60,000 acres, and 485 with more than 60,000 acres. The figures for the richest and most populous province, Buenos Aires, show a decline in the number of very large landholdings between 1901 and 1914, but they also show that even in the latter year 771 owners held more than one fourth of all the land, whereas, at the other end of the scale, some 29,000 owners held only about one fiftieth of it.

The Immigrant Flood and Urbanization

Students of the history of the United States who recall how its liberal land system was a lure to immigrants may be surprised that Argentina, without any such system, attracted an even larger volume of immigration in proportion to its original population. Various explanations may be given, the simplest being that the immigrants to Argentina came for different reasons or else changed their minds after arriving there. But whatever the explanation, the fact remains that Argentina has been one of the world's leading countries of immigration in modern times. Argentina's influx of immigrants reached its all-time peak in the period under consideration in the present chapter; and by the end of that period in 1916 the immigrants and their offspring were already playing a notable role in the economic, social, and political life of the country.

In the peak period of the world's oversea migration, 1821-1932, six countries absorbed 90 per cent of the total, and among these six

* 1 hectare = 2.47 acres.

Argentina ranked second in number of immigrants, with a total of 6,405,000. The only other Latin American country in the list is Brazil, with 4,431,000. The United States, of course, came first with about five times as many as Argentina, but, as already noted, the latter's immigration was more intense in relation to its native population. This is apparent from a comparison of the proportion of foreign-born to total population in the two countries. In Argentina, the foreign-born made up 25.5 per cent of the population in 1895 and 30.3 per cent in 1914, which was more than twice as high as the highest proportion ever reached in the United States (14.4 per cent in 1890 and again in 1910). And we may note that the Argentine figure has remained more than twice as high as the United States' ever since: in 1950 the proportions were 15.7 per cent in Argentina and 6.7 per cent in the United States.

Argentine immigration statistics began to be kept only in 1857 and at first there was little to record. As late as the decade 1871-1880 the net immigration (excess of arrivals over departures) averaged only 8,500 per year. Then came a dramatic change: the rate increased nearly eightfold for the decade 1881-1890, during which the total number of immigrants was 638,000. With the hard times of the 1890s the figure for that decade dropped back to 320,000, but even that was far in excess of anything known before 1880. In 1901-1910 prosperity returned and the immigrant total was the highest in Argentina's whole history, 1,120,000. The sum total for the three decades was 2,078,000, as compared with a total national population of less than two million at the first census in 1869. The volume remained high until it was greatly reduced by the outbreak of war in Europe in 1914.

The chief sources of immigration to Argentina have always been Italy and Spain; from 1857 to 1958 they accounted for 46 and 33 per cent respectively of the total immigration. Between 1881 and 1900 the Italians outnumbered the Spaniards about 3 to 1, but the latter drew abreast in the next decade and far ahead in the war decade that followed. The remainder of the immigrants (21 per cent) were made up of an assortment of nationalities, including French, German, Swiss, British, and Irish; there were even a few from the United States. Though their numbers were small, these minority immigrant groups averaged high in special skills and soon achieved distinction in their new homes. To give only two examples, a Frenchman, Paul Groussac, became one of Argentina's leading men of letters, and a German, Wilhelm Kraft, founded a publishing firm that soon became, as it still is, a leader in its field in Argentina.

Most of the immigrants came from the poorer classes of society; until 1890 three fourths of them came from rural areas; and in Argentina they started out as laborers, urban or rural. Indeed, half of the gross immigration was made up of seasonal workers or "swallows" (*golondrinas*), who crossed the Atlantic only to work the Southern Hemisphere harvest season in Argentina and then recrossed it for the Northern Hemisphere harvest season at home. In many cases, however, the immigrants either already had or soon achieved middle-class status, whether as small businessmen, shopkeepers, artisans, office workers, or members of the liberal professions. Studies based on census figures for 1895 and 1914 show that at a time when the foreign-born made up 39 and 47 per cent respectively of the working population, they provided a much larger proportion (from two thirds to four fifths) of the commercial and industrial entrepreneurs, slightly more than half the personnel of the liberal professions in 1895 (and slightly less in 1914), and somewhat more than half the commercial office workers. On the other hand, they held well under one third of the government office jobs (being political ciphers, they had no claim on political patronage), and furnished only ten per cent of the landowners and only about one third of the domestic servants but from 50 to 60 per cent of the industrial workers. The sons of the immigrants sometimes rose to high political office even before 1912; the outstanding example is, of course, Carlos Pellegrini.

The immigrants found it easier to get ahead in the city than in the country, and easier in agriculture than in stockraising. The acquisition of land was made difficult for them not only by the land system but also by the tenacity with which the native Argentines held on to their properties, whether because of the great social prestige of landowning or for some other reason. As a result, in rural areas relatively few of the foreign-born ever rose above the status of tenant or salaried manager. Even as common laborers they had only limited opportunities in stockraising, especially when the stock were horses and cattle. This was the most traditional Argentine way of life, and it acquired a new glamour when the beef barons became the rulers, and their *estancias* the symbols, of the thriving new Argentina. Even in the city of Buenos Aires the most elite institution was the Rural Society, founded in 1866, whose annual, week-long cattle expositions in suburban Palermo were, until Perón's time, the greatest events of the year for all classes alike. And in between expositions the Society's influence on the life of the nation was, we are told on good authority, immeasurable. Accordingly, when the emergence of the new Argentina upset old ways, the tradition-bound rural classes gravitated toward the stock farms, where life had changed least. Agriculture, which did not have this traditional pull, therefore offered the foreign-born better opportunities. Here they played a decisive part in the great expansion of grain-growing in the late nineteenth and early twentieth centuries, though, as noted above, ownership remained vested mainly in native Argentines, many of whom were absentee landlords.

One consequence of this state of affairs was the concentration of the foreign-born in two areas: first, in the cities, above all Buenos Aires, and second, in the principal areas of agricultural production, which included the provinces of the littoral, from Buenos Aires through Santa Fe to Entre Ríos, and also Córdoba, La Pampa, and Mendoza. In these two areas the foreign-born made up from 39 to 52 per cent of the total population in 1895, and from 41 to 49 per cent in 1914. In all the rest of the country, on the other hand, the proportion of foreign-born to total population was only 9 and 10 per cent respectively in the same years.

A further consequence was the stimulus given by the immigrant stock to the urbanization of Argentina. The Argentine definition of an urban community as one containing at least 2,000 inhabitants is a rather generous one, but as it has been used for many years it at least provides a fixed standard of comparison. By this standard, the urban sector of Argentina's population doubled between 1869 and 1914, rising from 27 per cent in 1869 through 37 per cent in 1895 to 53 per cent in 1914. Most striking of all was the growth of the city of Buenos Aires, which was twice as rapid as that of the nation at large. In 1869 the city's metropolitan area had 230,000 inhabitants, or just over one eighth of the national total; in 1914 it had 2,035,000, or just over one fourth of the whole. The city's growth was due in large part to immigration from abroad, for 49 per cent of its inhabitants in 1914 were foreign-born. Migration from the interior, which was later to become a major factor, accounted for only 11 per cent of its population in 1914.

In addition to their part in the nation's development in other ways, such as business, the professions, agriculture, and urbanization, Argentina's immigrant stock played a highly important political role. This had two aspects. First, there was the influence of the immigrants, and still more of their first-generation offspring, in bringing about the peaceful political revolution of 1916. To be sure, it resulted from a reform movement whose leadership and ideology were traditionally Argentine. But the oligarchy successfully resisted until forced to surrender, without striking a blow, by the growth of a massive Radical party based on a new middle class, both of which were growths of a soil laid down by the immigrant flood.

In the second place, to many native Argentines, the immigrants themselves were a political problem of the first magnitude. Even Sarmiento, once foremost in bidding them come, had serious misgivings about them late in life. Buenos Aires, already half foreign-born, he called "a city without citizens," and continued:

> The most industrious and progressive of its 400,000 inhabitants are strangers here who . . . remain unchanged in their roles as instruments, makers, builders. . . . We shall build, if we have not already built, a Tower of Babel in America, its workmen speaking all tongues, not blending them together. . . . One does not construct a homeland without patriotism . . . nor does one build . . . a city without citizens.

The things that disturbed Sarmiento about the foreigners—their materialism, their alien tongues, their lack of civic spirit and patriotism—gave increasing concern as their numbers grew. While it was too early for a reversal of the long-established open-door immigration policy, the concern expressed itself in a number of other ways. One was the Law of Residence of 1902, aimed against foreign agitators; another, an upsurge of creole nationalism, of which more will be said below.

There was ground for concern, but it turned out to be exaggerated. The sheer magnitude of the problem of assimilating or fusing so great a mass of aliens was frightening, but on the other hand the great majority of them, those from Italy and Spain, were not so very alien. Only the Italians presented a language problem and time solved this: the second generation spoke Spanish. Another thing that disturbed native Argentines was the multiplicity of voluntary associations formed by the aliens, which seemed to set up an institutional wall between them and the rest of the nation. Some of these associations were confined to a single nationality, while others included more than one but still were overwhelmingly foreign. The second, or "cosmopolitan," type of association preponderated in Buenos Aires, the first type in the rest of the country. In 1914 the two types together numbered about 1,500, one third of which were in Buenos Aires. They engaged in a variety of activities, social, fraternal, protective, and educational, and included most of the labor unions, in which Anarchists predominated before 1914, with the Socialists far behind in second place. If for a time these associations justified the fears of nationalists, they represented a natural reaction on the part of aliens excluded from active participation in the political life of the country. In the long run, concludes a recent student, they made a positive contribution to national unity as the linguistic and political barriers between their members and the rest of the nation were removed.

Perhaps the most important single factor in the assimilation or fusion of the immigrant stock was one noted above in another connection, namely the fact that as early as the 1890s a great many immigrants had already been integrated individually into the life of the nation in one occupation or another, whether as farm or factory worker, businessman, physician, or lawyer. Moreover, many of the immigrants felt little if any attachment to the old country and were quite ready to take on the ways of their new homeland. By way of illustration: when the cult of that most traditional Argentine figure, the gaucho, caught on about the turn of the century, its converts included Italian as well as Spanish immigrants, and one of their children's favorite street games in Buenos Aires was playing gaucho. In fact, it was not so much the immigrants' reluctance to join as it was the oligarchy's unwillingness to admit them on terms of equality that kept them from becoming full-fledged members of the Argentine nation. It was easy for them to acquire citizenship by naturalization after only two years' residence, but they would be second-class citizens, for they could still neither vote nor hold office, and naturalization would only subject them to compulsory military service. As a result, the vast majority of foreign-born residents remained aliens; in 1914 only 2.3 per cent of them had been naturalized in Buenos Aires, and less than half that many in the rest of the country.

Although the problem of assimilating the immigrants was never quite so formidable as apprehensive Argentines thought, it was never completely solved for them, but only for their sons. Even for the latter the solution stopped short with the incorporation of immigrants of the middle class as full-fledged citizens, leaving the immigrant masses in a kind of political and social limbo. Native Argentines at the foot of the social ladder fared likewise, and the two groups combined to form a new syncretism, with consequences that did not become fully apparent until the Perón era three decades later.

Education, Culture, and Nationalism

As already noted, a strong impulse was given public education by Mitre, Sarmiento, and Avellaneda, and the rate of literacy rose from 22 per cent in 1869 to 65 per cent in 1914, a level not yet reached by most Latin American countries a half century later. In accordance with the oligarchy's general program of modernizing the country, religious instruction and Latin were eliminated from the public school curriculum. Many Argentines resented these changes. One critic, writing many years later, commented sourly that "without history, without the catechism, and without classical instruction, the rupture with tradition was complete." His generalization was misleading in at least one respect, for Argentine history of a sort was taught. Writing in 1894, Agustín Alvarez complained that it was taught in such a way as to instill into the rising generation an "exaggerated belief in the glory and destiny of their country." But, as we shall see, Ricardo Rojas had other ideas.

Higher education, concentrated at first in the universities of Córdoba and Buenos Aires, still performed its traditional function of preparing young men for the professions. Besides its faculties of Law and Medicine, the University of Buenos Aires had faculties of Engineering and (added in the 1890s) Philosophy and Letters, and its School of Law included "and Social Sciences" in its name. Unfriendly critics complained, however, that this school's only important function was to turn out lawyers capable of serving the oligarchy's interlocking interests in government, agriculture, and foreign trade. Such judgments depended on the point of view. As seen by a Law School graduate and gold medalist of 1898, the University of Buenos Aires was Argentina's "supreme cultural institution"; its Law School enjoyed "very high social and intellectual prestige" and attracted outstanding jurists, lawyers, and statesmen to its faculty; and the students were eager young men who never tired of discussing problems of the classroom and public life.

A new departure was made with the founding of the University of La Plata (1906), with Joaquín V. González as its rector. González, who won distinction both as writer and as statesman, was a conservative who felt the need for renovation. Consulting experts in Europe and the United States, including Leo S. Rowe, then of the University of Pennsylvania, he planned his new university along what were then ultramodern lines, which included stress on the sciences. This was only one sign of a deep discontent with the country's whole system of higher education. Others, far more radical than González, were to launch in 1918 a movement for a sweeping reform of the universities.

The intellectual life of most of the period was dominated by the so-called Generation of Eighty (1880). Made up of men whose careers began about that year, and concentrated in the city of Buenos Aires, this generation had a wide variety of interests and sympathies, but in the main its ideas were those of European positivism and its policies those of the Argentine oligarchy. They were cosmopolitan in the sense that they took Europe as their literary, philosophical, and artistic model. In the 1880s they even set out to convert Buenos Aires physically into the Paris of South America, plowing the new Avenida de Mayo through the heart of the city, as a local equivalent of the Champs-Élysées. And they were liberal in the sense that they championed individualism and personal rights, especially free speech and free enterprise; though at the same time they accepted the oligarchy's view that, in Argentina, limited democracy was necessary because the masses were not yet qualified to share in the exercise of political power.

In one version or another, European positivism enjoyed a great vogue throughout Latin America in the late nineteenth and early twentieth centuries. All the principal versions were present in Argentina, but with widely different degrees of effectiveness. Auguste Comte's teachings, so influential in neighboring Brazil, found only limited acceptance in Argentina because of their antiliberal, religious, and "sociocratic" or communitarian character. On the other hand, social Darwinism was warmly welcomed in high circles for the support it gave the thesis of "limited democracy." But the most influential philosopher in Argentina was Herbert Spencer, whose liberalism and individualism, it was believed, would be most conducive to the development of the kind of civilization envisaged by Argentine positivists: one in which a maximum of wealth would be produced by giving free play to individual initiative. James Bryce, writing particularly about Argentina and Chile, noted that "the European books most popular among the few who approach abstract subjects are those of Herbert Spencer. . . . Those few," he added, wryly, "are unwilling to believe that he is not deemed in his own country [England] to be a great philosopher."

As already suggested, these views were not shared by all the members of the Generation of Eighty. Indeed, one of the most distinguished of them, Juan Agustín García, dissented violently. Spencer's influence on Argentina was disastrous, he charged, for it had helped to turn the country into "one colossal *estancia*, bristling with railroads and canals, full of workshops, with populous cities, abounding in riches of all kinds, but without a single learned man, artist, or philosopher." Tired of so much aping of Europe, García urged his fellow countrymen to turn back to their own past for light and learning. Joaquín González was another early exponent of nativism. Still others undertook a re-evaluation of Juan Manuel de Rosas and reported that he was not simply the xenophobe tyrant of the orthodox histories but a complex man who embodied some of the best and most characteristic Argentine traits.

Toward the close of the period, and especially in connection with the centenary of independence in 1910, a new generation of writers carried the cult of nativism still further, merging it with nationalism. It is no mere coincidence that in these same years the generation-old gaucho poem *Martín Fierro* acquired an unprecedented vogue and became enshrined as a national classic. The leaders of this generation wrote in various forms—poetry, philosophy, history, sociology, biography, novels, essays—and disagreed with one another on many

points, but all were fervent nationalists. The centenary was hailed by
Leopoldo Lugones with an "Ode to the Herds and Grain-fields," and
by Ricardo Rojas with a book, *The Nationalist Restoration*. A few
years later Rojas developed his nationalist thought still further in
another book called simply *La Argentinidad*, which may be loosely
rendered as "One Hundred Per Cent Argentinism." Manuel Gálvez,
too, saluted the centenary with what proved to be the first of a long
line of nationalist books, mostly novels. And José Ingenieros, founder
in 1915 of an important journal, *Revista de Filosofía*, and said to
have been in his prime the most widely read of all writers in Spanish, celebrated the emergence of an "Argentine white race" and
called on it to play a tutelary role of "pacific imperialism" over the
rest of South America.

Like all expressions of nationalism, Argentina's had its roots in
Europe. This was most evident in the works of Ricardo Rojas, which
contain unmistakable echoes of the German high priest of romantic
nationalism in the early nineteenth century, Herder. Yet early twentieth-century Argentine nationalism was necessarily in part anti-
European. Rojas, for example, aimed his sharpest shafts against
Argentina's "cosmopolitanism," by which he meant first and foremost
its cultural subordination to Europe. This he proposed to end by a
nationalist campaign beginning in the schools with the teaching of
history, which must be reformed to eliminate the "poison" of cosmopolitanism and promote patriotism. As he used the term, it also
meant the economic domination of Argentina by European and other
foreign capital and business enterprise; and he called on his fellow
countrymen to throw off this yoke too.

Foreign Relations

Argentina's foreign relations from 1880 to 1916 were conditioned
by its domestic political, economic, and cultural development as
described above. Nationalism notwithstanding, its already strong ties
with England and continental Europe were greatly strengthened.
As long as the dominant oligarchy remained in power these were
most unlikely to be weakened, for the oligarchy was in effect the
agent of the estancieros, who were both the principal Argentine beneficiaries of this state of affairs and also doubly dependent on Europe.
They depended on it absolutely for a market, since at that time there

was no conceivable alternative. They also depended on it almost as completely for capital investments, since they spent most of their handsome profits on conspicuous consumption and invested abroad what little capital they accumulated. The United States was barely beginning to offer an alternative to Europe at the close of the period: it was itself a debtor nation until World War I; and in any case Argentine habits and preferences favored the maintenance of the European bias.

In fact, throughout this period Argentina belonged to the European system rather than to that American system which leaders in the United States had been talking about since the time of Thomas Jefferson, Henry Clay, and James Monroe. This was made clear by Roque Saenz Peña's famous speech at the Pan American Conference of 1890, in which he explained his rejection of Blaine's all-American customs union plan by saying, "I cannot forget that in Europe are Spain our mother; Italy, our friend; and France, our elder sister." Frankness would have required him to add, "and Britain, our chief financier and trading partner."

This spirit of aloofness from special American ties did not become exacerbated with the passing years, but neither did it decline. In 1902 Foreign Minister Luis M. Drago made a tentative move toward inter-American involvement with his "Drago Doctrine," which was a kind of financial and economic corollary to the Monroe Doctrine; but this was soon reversed by his government. At the close of the Fourth Inter-American Conference, held in Buenos Aires in 1910, that city's newspaper *La Nación* probably expressed the views of most of its people when it commented that the conference had shown that the Latin Americans were neither Europeans nor North Americans, but Argentines or Brazilians or Cubans. Yet Latin America as well as the United States was held at arm's length by the Argentines in power. When Theodore Roosevelt visited Buenos Aires in 1913, their foreign minister declared at a meeting in Roosevelt's honor that, if they regarded Pan Americanism as impractical, they also took little interest in Latin American countries that were farther away than Hamburg or Geneva. "We cannot cultivate this [American] sentiment," said he, "by destroying the bonds that unite us with Europe."

The fact is that Argentina adhered closely to her long-standing policy of modified isolationism throughout this period. The policy favored bilateral but not multilateral commitments, and it was reinforced by Argentina's enduring passion for peace engendered by the costly Paraguayan War of 1865-70. Under the oligarchy, her growing wealth and power ended Brazil's preponderance in the River Plate region and led to a satisfactory settlement of a dangerous boundary dispute with Chile in 1902. Then, a decade later, Argentina formed with these two the "A.B.C. bloc," but this was only a loose entente, not an alliance. Noninvolvement and peace were still her passion. So, when Europe went to war in 1914, Argentina declared her neutrality, though the nominally Anglophil oligarchy was still in power. She was still neutral when Radical President Irigoyen, certainly no friend to England, took office in 1916.

FOUR

RADICALS IN POWER:
THE LIGHT THAT FAILED
1916-1930

More than half the Argentine people rejoiced over Radical leader Hipólito Irigoyen's election in 1916 as a victory over the forces of darkness and the dawn of a new era. Yet there was also great rejoicing in 1930 when, after fourteen years of Radical domination, Irigoyen and his demoralized party were ousted by a handful of soldiers and a whiff of grapeshot. In the interval the Radicals had fulfilled so little of the promise of 1916 that their record could have been summed up as a failure even if their fall had not been so ignominious and definitive.

The reasons for the Radicals' failure challenge inquiry, for, when united, they have always formed the largest party in Argentina. Moreover, theirs is the party of the Argentine middle class, which is the largest such class in any Latin American country, numbering some 30 per cent of the total population by 1914 and 40 per cent a generation later. Finally, in a modernized, urbanized society such as Argentina's, the middle class might be expected to play a dominant role in politics.

The explanation offered below may be summarized in three points: (1) Personalism, which is usually a major factor in Latin American politics, was decisive in this case. The Radical party in the period in question rose with Irigoyen and fell with him. (2) Twenty-odd years of adherence to their motto of "abstention and revolution" had left the Radicals ill prepared for the task of government. Abstention resulted in a lack of experienced personnel and the negative character

65

of the party's motto failed to provide it with a corporate sense of direction. The latter deficiency, intensified and made permanent by Irigoyen's persistent refusal to adopt a program, turned the party into a self-serving machine. (3) In the absence of agreed common objectives, each of the Radical party's component social groups more and more followed its own bent, and they were highly heterogeneous. Most of the members belonged to the so-called middle class, but that class itself lacked unity, and in addition there were also members who belonged to the upper and lower classes. Hence the party was increasingly unable to form a consensus of its own, much less to meet the greatest need of the new Argentina: the need for a new national consensus.

Radical Administrations

Argentine practice makes the pattern of presidential administrations more meaningful in the history of that country than it is in the case of the United States, despite the close similarity between the two countries' constitutions and forms of government. The presidential pattern provides a particularly appropriate framework for the history of the period of Radical domination in Argentina. The pattern is a simple one: first Irigoyen, then Marcelo T. de Alvear, each for the constitutional term of six years; then Irigoyen again, for a term cut short after two years by revolution.

Grandson of an executed Rosista who was Leandro Alem's father, Irigoyen was born on July 12, 1852, five months after the battle of Caseros toppled Rosas' regime. He was therefore sixty-four years old at the time of his first inauguration, on October 12, 1916. The scene that day was typical both of the man and of his relation to the masses. As he was on his way to the inauguration, in the horse-drawn presidential carriage, some of the admiring crowd unhitched the horses, took their places, and pulled the carriage with its occupant to the appointed place a mile or so away through wildly cheering throngs that packed the streets and plazas. All the while Irigoyen acknowledged their cheers courteously but with grave impassivity. He was not a rabble-rouser, never harangued a crowd, and seldom spoke in public; even his messages to Congress were not delivered in person. Perhaps this was just as well, for his literary style was abominable: inflated, pretentious, obscure, a mixture of mysticism and nonsense, with a strong dose of the Krausist philosophy so highly esteemed in certain Spanish and Spanish American circles at that time.* Yet if his writings often did not make sense, they created an image of the man that was of inestimable political value, for to those who did not detest Irigoyen—no one in Argentina was neutral about him—they seemed full of lofty sentiments and made him appear as deeply devoted to Argentina and the common people, "the real Argentines," as he was hostile to the oligarchs who, according to him, exploited both country and people.

But Irigoyen was at his best in private conversation. Life-long practice had made him a past master in the art of conspiracy; but there was much more to it than that. He could be charming even in his dealings with political enemies from whom he could not hope to gain anything. One of them, Carlos Ibarguren, recalls how at their only meeting, which had to do with official business about a historical monument, President Irigoyen received him with extreme affability and spoke simply and warmly in a style far superior to that of his public speeches, though still employing some of his most characteristic terms, saying "cause" for party, and "creed" for platform or program. At the end he granted more than Ibarguren had asked for, escorted him to the door, and dismissed him with an effusive handshake. "A singularly attractive personality," concluded his visitor, who went on to note that physically, too, Irigoyen was quite out of the ordinary: tall, relaxed, dark-complexioned, with features that suggested the Orient, especially in his more solemn moments, when he looked like an enigmatic Buddha.

"Enigmatic" is the key word here, for it is the only one that will unlock the mystery of his magnetism. He was conspicuously lacking in most of the attributes one first thinks of as charismatic in the Argentine society of his day. It was a society that worshiped wealth, but he lived simply all his days and gave his salary as president to charity. Yet on the other hand he never made the appeal of poverty; though his wants were simple, he never wanted for anything. For many years a schoolteacher, he made a good but not very dignified living by "moonlighting" as a *ganadero* or stockraiser on rented *estancias*. In a society that also glorified the *macho* or he-man, he was neither a military hero (as Roca had been), nor a super-gaucho

* The reference is to the German philosopher Karl C. F. Krause (1781-1832).

(as Rosas had been), nor a sexual athlete: he apparently had several liaisons in his long life, but his prowess in this respect was not extraordinary. And besides being no rabble-rouser, he made ruthless use of military force to break a general strike midway in his first administration, and conferred few substantial benefits on the workers.

That Irigoyen nevertheless dominated Argentine public life in the 1920s, winning his greatest triumph at the polls in 1928, remains a mystery unless it is explained by the aura of mystery with which he surrounded himself. By dint of decades of persistent revolutionary activity, which, like an iceberg, lay mostly beneath the surface, he got himself recognized as a man with a vaguely great mission. He gave it a strongly religious character by tireless repetition of such terms as cause, creed, and "apostolate," and by making an imperative claim on his followers' faith. Only a few of his goals were explicitly stated and most of these were achieved by the time he took office, some through the electoral reform law of 1912, and others by the mere fact of his first election. This success added greatly to public faith in his apostolate.

Just how Irigoyen proposed to use power, he never made clear. He had always refused to commit himself and his party to a program, and success served only to add a note of arrogance to the refusal. Just after his abortive revolt of 1905, he issued a manifesto in which he said: "The Unión Cívica Radical is not properly speaking a party in the militant sense; it is a conjunction of forces emerging from the opinion of the nation, [forces] born from and solidified by the heat of public demands." In 1909 he said it would be the "gravest and most fatal error" for the Radicals to become such a party, and that that was precisely the error its enemies were trying to trick it into by demanding that it define its program. After victory, he discovered that the demand was sheer impertinence, an effort on the losers' part to tie the Radicals' hands.

All this was not mere mystification. It served Irigoyen's apostolate well in at least two ways: it permitted him to concentrate on the tactical maneuvers of practical politics, at which he was very good indeed; and it provided a wide latitude of hope to the many discordant elements that made up the Radical party. The latter consideration was particularly important for a number of reasons: because the character of the party had already changed by 1916 through the addition of more and more sons of immigrants to the party's original creole base represented by Alem and by Irigoyen himself; because the diversity increased after the Radicals' successes at the polls following the electoral reform of 1912 attracted new recruits to the bandwagon; and because once the original bond of unity, determination to oust the oligarchy, had been achieved, the party was in danger of flying apart if its policy on major issues were too clearly defined and pushed with too much vigor. This danger was real and it soon materialized in spite of all Irigoyen could do to avert it.

This is not to say that his first administration was devoid of either direction or achievements, but only that he moved with great circumspection behind a smoke-screen of moralistic pronouncements that meant different things to different people. The record of this administration can be reviewed best by taking up successively its foreign and domestic aspects. In both, his most enduring contribution was the impulse he gave to Argentine nationalism.

Since Irigoyen took office in the midst of World War I, foreign affairs dominated the early years of his first administration. He adhered firmly to a policy of neutrality throughout, against considerable pressure from both domestic and foreign quarters and in the face of provocations by Germany. To be sure, neutrality had been the policy of his conservative predecessor, but Irigoyen maintained it after the United States became a belligerent in April 1917, when a conservative government might conceivably have entered the war, as Brazil and several other Latin American countries did. What is more, Irigoyen tried to promote neutralism in Latin America at large and called a conference to that end. The effort failed through opposition from Latin American sources as well as from the United States, but it is interesting as an anticipation of Juan Perón's "Third Position" in its application to foreign policy. Although Irigoyen's course was widely attributed at the time to pro-Germanism, it would seem to have been rather an authentic expression of Argentine nationalism. For one thing, he did not want his country to be drawn into the war as a satellite of the United States. For another, while there is no evidence that he worked for a German victory, he probably hoped that Germany would not be so badly beaten as to increase Argentina's already

excessive dependence on Great Britain, with which his conservative
opponents were economically and socially allied.

The most striking evidence that Irigoyen was not pro-German came
when reports were circulated that Germany was plotting, with the
aid of the large German colony in southern Brazil, to invade Uruguay,
which was pro-Ally. Irigoyen responded to these reports in February
1918 with a promise of Argentine support of Uruguay against any
such invasion. This promise has also been adduced as evidence of
his devotion to the principle of Latin American solidarity. He did
indeed express such sentiments, and he went on to declare that,
united, the Latin American nations would constitute "one of the most
powerful entities in the world." Yet at the same time, in a passage
that provides a fair sample of his macaronic literary style, he explicitly
based his action on "my American creed" and defined this as devotion to "the fundamental maintenance of the sovereignty of nations
in its immanent and immutable consecration, as decreed by divine
Providence and crowned by the spirit of each of them." Whatever
else this curious passage may mean, it leaves no doubt that Irigoyen
was first and foremost a nationalist. In the same spirit, at the end
of his administration he rejected overtures from Brazil and Chile for
a limitation-of-arms agreement among these three "great powers" of
South America.

Finally, as regards the League of Nations, Irigoyen first joined the
new body so as not to be left out and then, when certain changes
in its charter proposed by Argentina were not immediately discussed,
severed active connection with the League, though without completely withdrawing from it. Some of his proposals had merit, such
as those which would have established universality of membership
and the complete equality of all member states. Moreover, Irigoyen's
admirers have contrasted his course favorably with that of the
United States, which never joined the League at all. It would seem,
however, that Irigoyen would have given better proof of his devotion
to principle if he had kept his country in the League at least long
enough to make a good fight for his proposals. In this case, too, he
showed himself first and foremost an Argentine nationalist, and an
isolationist. Argentine tradition, though not unbroken, was mainly on
his side.

Economic and Social Problems

Domestic and foreign policy overlapped at many points under Irigoyen. The overlapping was greatest in the economic field, for his nationalism found one of its chief expressions in resistance to foreign economic penetration of Argentina. Again tradition was on his side, for Rosas had made such resistance a prominent feature of his regime in the 1830s and '40s. Though slighted after Rosas' fall amid the enthusiasm for a policy of economic development with foreign aid that was brilliantly successful in many ways, the theme had never lacked advocates. Foremost among these was the founder of the Socialist party, Juan B. Justo, but they also included traditionalist republicans such as Bernardo de Irigoyen (no kin to Hipólito) and even that pillar of the oligarchy, Carlos Pellegrini, who, at the very zenith of Argentina's Gilded Age in the 1880s, took his fellow countrymen to task for their dependence on foreign financing.

The theme, then, was not new when Irigoyen took it up, but he was the first Argentine president to give it prominence, sustained support on a broad front, and practical application. He therefore merits an important niche in history as a forerunner of the fully developed economic nationalism of the Perón period. Irigoyen's variety of it, however, was mild and elementary compared not only with Perón's a generation later, but even with those of his own contemporaries in Mexico and Uruguay. While Irigoyen sounded the nationalist note in season and out, and applied it verbally to a wide range of topics, including petroleum, railroads, packing plants, and land ownership, he translated his doctrine into action in only one major instance, involving petroleum, and one minor instance, involving land ownership.

Irigoyen's major blow for Argentine economic independence was the establishment of the national petroleum agency, Y.P.F.,* in 1922. Large petroleum deposits had been discovered some fifteen years earlier, near Comodoro Rivadavia on the coast of south central Argentina. Legislation to protect the national interest in them had already been adopted, but Irigoyen's administration was the first

* Yacimientos Petrolíferos Fiscales, or Fiscal (i.e., Government) Petroleum Deposits.

to set up a national organization for their development. Y.P.F. was also given exclusive control of any new oil fields that might be discovered thereafter, though without disturbing previously established private companies. Its creation is a landmark in the history of Argentine public policy for two reasons: first, because it gave effective expression for the first time to Irigoyen's principle that public utilities should be controlled not by private enterprise, either foreign or domestic, but by the state; and second, because Y.P.F. became one of the most jealously guarded symbols of Argentine economic independence.

The person chosen to direct the new Y.P.F. was an army officer, Colonel Carlos Mosconi, who according to all accounts performed admirably.* Thereafter, as the government's role in the economy expanded, it drew increasingly on the military for technical experts. Apparently it did so because the best talent of this kind was produced by the institutes and academies of the armed forces, which had been reorganized and professionalized since the turn of the century. We shall have more to say about this later on.

Irigoyen also undertook a land reform which he and his admirers regarded as a notable achievement, but which in retrospect seems to have fallen considerably short of that. The lands affected totalled about 20 million acres, but they lay for the most part on the outer periphery of the country's settled area, about equally divided between northern and southern Argentina. Whatever the merits of his effort, it skirted the main problem, for the great bulk of the Argentine economy, rural as well as urban-industrial, continued to be concentrated in areas that his reforms left untouched. It was almost as if Lincoln's Emancipation Proclamation had not been followed by a Union victory and the adoption of the Thirteenth Amendment.

For the rest, Irigoyen's economic policy, particularly in regard to foreign capital investments and business enterprise in Argentina, was remarkably similar to that of his conservative predecessors. He left the Argentine economy almost exactly as he found it: a one-sided agrarian economy controlled in large measure by foreign interests and dependent on the sale of its cereals and meats in a foreign market.

* Mosconi's appointment was made at the beginning of the term of Irigoyen's successor, Alvear.

Why there was such a wide gap between Irigoyen's principles and his practice is not difficult to understand, but the reasons were many. To begin with the most obvious, he was, as already noted, primarily a moralist in his approach to public issues. He knew little about economics; and so, when confronted by the issue of foreign economic penetration, he took hold of it at its Argentine end, the oligarchy, whose corrupt alliance with foreign exploiters of the people provided him with a fine moral handle.

Moreover, in the Argentina of that day it was politically more rewarding to concentrate one's fire on the domestic oligarchs, as Irigoyen did, rather than on their foreign allies. This was partly because the oligarchs were easier to reach, but another reason has been suggested by a recent writer, Ernesto Palacio, who, while hostile to the oligarchy, is critical of Irigoyen as well. As he explains the situation, once the Radical party had won, foreign business interests began to court it, and leading Radical lawyers and businessmen, forgetting their principles for personal profit, scrambled for well paid posts as legal counsel or agents of one kind or another for the foreigners, who controlled most of the big business in Argentina. This intensified the Radicals' aversion for the oligarchy, whose professional henchmen were their chief rivals for such plums, but at the same time it restrained them from attacking the foreign business interests that distributed the plums.

Still another consideration, and one of a less invidious kind, must be added. The glamour of Argentina's remarkably rapid growth with foreign aid in the prewar generation still persisted, and the postwar decade promised a re-enactment of that happy scene. Down to 1928 the two principal ingredients of the earlier formula for success were repeated on a large scale: foreign investments boomed once more, and so did immigration from abroad. Even Radical leaders—who, it should be remembered, came mainly from the middle and upper-middle class—could hardly be blamed for welcoming the resumption of a tried-and-true process of national growth. It was easy to assume that some of the benefits would trickle down to the less fortunate strata of society.

In the realm of social development the Irigoyen administration's record was similarly mixed. On the one hand his earnest advocacy of justice for the common man helped to arouse the social conscience of the nation. Despite the essentially middle-class character of his party, he acquired something of a reputation as a man of the people —a characterization more likely to gain assent in upper-class circles than among the masses. In the same sense historians have called him the Andrew Jackson of Argentina; his administration did at any rate bring about an irruption of rough-hewn popular elements into public offices hitherto reserved for the well-educated, the well-born, and the well-to-do. Also, it may well be that his combination of humanitarianism and nationalism aided in the conversion of Argentine labor from internationalism and anarchism to identification with the nation and trade unionism. On the other hand, he gave only limited support to piecemeal social reforms and organized labor, although social and labor problems were multiplying, in city and countryside alike, with the rapid progress of both commercialized agriculture and urbanization, in a country flooded with immigrants.

Irigoyen's attitude toward both labor and social problems is illustrated by his position during and after the Tragic Week of January 1919. During the previous two years the number of strikes had grown rapidly as the cost of living skyrocketed; in 1918 the anarchist and syndicalist agitators already on hand were joined by communist agents from Russia, where the Bolsheviks had taken over late in 1917; and Argentine employers had countered by forming antilabor organizations such as the Patriotic League, which undertook to combat the extremists by rallying all good Argentines against them under the national flag. Tension mounted until in January 1919 a strike of metallurgical workers in Buenos Aires started a chain reaction of violence: intervention by the police, a clash between police and workers, a general strike, mob violence that terrorized the city for two days, and the spread of violence from Buenos Aires to Rosario, now the nation's second largest city.

At this point Irigoyen intervened, not only calling on the armed forces to restore order, but also authorizing business firms to organize private strong-arm squads. Order was restored and the strike broken, but thereafter Irigoyen's only effort to get at the root of the trouble was the adoption of his piecemeal reforms—relating to such matters as hours of labor and job security—which benefited only a fraction of the urban labor force, and above all the so-called aristocracy of labor. Prominent among the beneficiaries were the railway workers, and Irigoyen's willingness to placate them could hardly have been diminished by the fact that the railways which employed the great majority of them were foreign-owned.

While it would be quite inaccurate to describe Irigoyen as a do-nothing in the social field, we can only agree with the recent judgment of Sergio Bagú, an Argentine specialist in the social history of his country, that Irigoyen neither made nor attempted to make any fundamental change in the economic and social structure of Argentina, and that he left the sources of power, as he had found them, in the hands of a landowning upper class, which continued as before to direct the nation's economy and orient its foreign policy.

Politics

In the realm of politics it was otherwise, for here Irigoyen had a definite program calling for extensive change and provided strong leadership in carrying it out. His program was quite simple in conception: to establish Radical control of all the political institutions in Argentina, provincial and municipal as well as national, with the direction concentrated in his own hands. A very large measure of success rewarded his efforts. He was recognized as the head of the party, or movement, as he preferred to call it, and down through 1928 there was a rapid and generally steady increase in Radical control over the country.

This success was achieved largely through lavish use of the central government's constitutional power to intervene in the provinces for certain purposes, including the maintenance of republican government. Convinced as he was of his moral superiority and that of his party to their opponents, Irigoyen had no qualms about intervening for partisan purposes: what was good for the Radicals, he was sure, was good for the country. His interventions never gave him complete control—otherwise he would not have intervened so often; but he never gave up. While similar use of the power had been made by Irigoyen's predecessors from the time of Urquiza, none had ever used it so extensively or systematically.

There were indeed Augean stables to be cleaned in some of the provinces, but however great that need may have been, Irigoyen's course had two unfortunate results. In the first place, it accentuated the already great concentration of power in Buenos Aires; by 1930

Argentina's nominally federal system had become in fact national or unitary. This distressed adherents of the Argentine equivalent of states' rights, and overtaxed the central government of a country never known for administrative aptitude. In the second place, it confirmed and strengthened the abuse of the power of intervention, so that any reform in this respect was henceforth a very remote possibility. Now that the abuse begun by the corrupt oligarchy had been repeated again and again by the democratic party of high moral principles, no effective remedy remained. None could be provided by the Argentine courts, for, following the opinions of courts and commentators in the United States, they held from the start that this question of intervention was a political one and hence not subject to judicial determination.

Yet Irigoyen did not govern despotically in either of his administrations. To label him a caudillo of the Rosas type, as has been done, is quite inaccurate. The independence of the judiciary was respected and, except in the matter of intervention, the opposition functioned freely most of the time. Indeed, freedom of the press continued to be given extraordinarily wide latitude under a Supreme Court interpretation, dating from 1866, of the constitutional provision that the national government should neither enact laws restricting freedom of the press nor establish federal jurisdiction thereon. In the court's view this meant that the federal government could not defend itself against any kind of attack through the press, including even incitement to revolution, but had to rely on the provincial governments for its defense in such cases. This may have been one of the reasons why Irigoyen made such extensive use of intervention to gain control of the provinces. In any event, the interpretation was reaffirmed by the courts time and again through 1928 and remained unaltered until it was reversed in 1932.

In this connection note should be taken of Argentina's justly renowned University Reform of 1918, which was political as well as educational in both intent and effect. Beginning at the traditional stronghold of Argentine conservatism, the University of Córdoba, this revolutionary reform spread first over the rest of the country and then to several other Latin American countries, with profound effects that are still being felt today. Carried out under the auspices of the Radical regime, the Argentine reform aimed at modernizing and nationalizing the curriculum, raising standards, purging the faculties of conservative as well as incompetent members, increasing the number of universities, making each university autonomous or independent of the government, and giving the student body a decisive or at least important voice in the university administration.

Despite numerous defects and ambivalences, the University Reform was followed by a rise in the level of performance and by 1930 Argentina's system of higher education was generally regarded as the best in Latin America. Also, the students now came preponderantly from the middle rather than the upper class and played a political role more consistently than before the reform. They had their own organizations, and while these were never monolithic, they most commonly aligned themselves with the major left-wing party, the Irigoyen Radicals; in Argentina, Communism was not yet an important factor, and the Socialists were a split splinter.

Alvear, Antipersonalism, and Prosperity

University Reform was one of the factors, though probably a minor one, in the schism that took place in the Radical party during the administration of Irigoyen's hand-picked successor, Marcelo T. de Alvear (1922-28). The major factors were personal and social; there was no head-on collision over policy questions, though one would probably have taken place had Irigoyen been less averse to committing himself to a specific program. That a schism occurred may seem surprising, since the seceding faction was led by Alvear, who had been a Radical for some thirty years and had long worked closely with Irigoyen—since 1918, as Minister to France. But such rifts are not rare. Perhaps the closest analogy is provided by the one between Theodore Roosevelt and William Howard Taft.

Unlike Roosevelt, however, Irigoyen never gave his successor a clear field by going abroad when his own term ended. All the evidence indicates that he expected to continue to run the Radical party and the country. The expectation was reasonable. Alvear had never shown himself to be very strong-willed, he had no great popular following, and he had lived abroad for several years past—he had even been elected president *in absentia*. Moreover, he was a member of the old oligarchy: that not uncommon phenomenon, a man of patrician family and inherited wealth who was nevertheless a philo-

sophical liberal. He was therefore a fine exhibit for the Radical
party, which claimed to represent not just the middle and lower
classes, but the whole Argentine people. As president, he would be
a good front man and caretaker but never a threat to Irigoyen's
power.

Things turned out differently from the very start, for Alvear insisted on picking his own cabinet. One of the key disagreements
involved the Ministry of War. For this post, Irigoyen's choice was
the general who had restored order during the Tragic Week of 1919;
but Alvear appointed General Agustín P. Justo, who had just completed with distinction an assignment as head of the Army War
College. It was personal disputes of this kind that started the party
schism and made the distinctive name of the schismatic group, Antipersonalist, highly appropriate. But since the label "Radical" had
acquired great political drawing-power, the new group retained it
as their substantive name, calling themselves Antipersonalist Radicals.

While policy differences between the two factions did exist, there
were few of any significance. The narrowness of the policy gap is
best illustrated by the fact that Alvear not only continued Irigoyen's
Y.P.F., but also chose its exceptionally able director, Colonel Carlos
Mosconi, and supported his vigorous development of it. Likewise,
Alvear's policies in regard to foreign investments, trade, labor relations, and social welfare differed from Irigoyen's only in matters of
detail. There was a basic similarity even in things left undone: protection for domestic manufactures was conspicuous by its absence
in both administrations. Alvear laid decidedly less verbal emphasis
on nationalism, but in practice the only important divergence consisted in his abandonment of his predecessor's not very vigorous
efforts to curb the power of the foreign-owned railways and to break
the foreign monopoly of river transportation in the Plata basin.

There were reasons why a substantial policy gap ought to have
opened up between the two Radical groups. In contrast to the left-
wing Irigoyenists, Alvear's Antipersonalists not only shared the
oligarchy's social conservatism and peculiar brand of economic liberalism but also formed a loose alliance with its representatives in
Congress against Irigoyen's wing. But Argentina's economic and
social development had not yet produced a nationally-oriented middle-
class group sufficiently strong and coherent to challenge seriously the

internationally-oriented policies best represented by the oligarchy and collectively labelled economic liberalism. Such a challenge had been thrown down long since by Socialists, and Irigoyen endorsed it, but, for reasons already suggested, he was not the man to translate it into a systematic program. Nor was any substantial part of the Argentine middle class yet ready to support the challenge. Many of its leading members—businessmen and professional men alike, and Irigoyenists as well as Antipersonalists—were in fact identified with the international economy, which provided them with good careers while prosperity lasted, as it did throughout Alvear's administration. Only when the happy days were ended by a series of seismic disturbances from 1929 to 1932—economic depression, revolution, dictatorship, restoration of the oligarchy—did a nationally oriented middle class, or "national bourgeoisie," begin to emerge as an influential factor in Argentine public life.

Radical Triumph and Rout

Shortly before the first of those earthquakes took place, Irigoyen returned to the Casa Rosada in triumph. The manner of his return once more demonstrated the completeness and personalist character of Irigoyen's political control. In 1922 he had got Alvear elected president *in absentia*; now, in 1928, almost effortlessly he overwhelmed Alvear's Antipersonalists and won re-election to the presidency by the widest margin, and in the most democratic election, in the history of Argentina. Although Irigoyen entered the race at the eleventh hour and did not bother to campaign, he received two thirds of the 1,200,000 popular votes and more than three fourths of the 316 electoral votes. Forty per cent of the adult male population voted in this election, as compared with thirty per cent in 1916 and only nine per cent in 1910. He was inaugurated on October 12. This is Columbus Day to some, but Irigoyen, following Spain's lead, designated it *el día de la raza*, or "Day of the Race," meaning the Spanish race: a gesture of Hispanic solidarity on the part of this traditionalist.

The very magnitude of Irigoyen's popular triumph helped prepare the way for his almost equally popular overthrow less than two years later. It did so partly by arousing inflated expectations which ended quickly in disillusionment and reaction, and partly by exacerbating the right-wing groups who had always opposed his regime bitterly.

Recently, they had been reinforced by antidemocratic contagions from abroad. These contagions included some that were widespread in the postwar Atlantic world, such as a decline of confidence in the political party system and representative democracy, and a corresponding rise of faith in the ability of the armed forces to bring about a political and moral regeneration. Others were of a more special character, such as those emanating from Benito Mussolini's fascist Italy, the quasi-fascist Spanish dictatorship of General Miguel Primo de Rivera, and the *Action Française* led by Charles Maurras. All these gave fresh strength to the hard core of irreconcilable anti-Radicals, which was made up mainly of the oligarchy, its civilian henchmen, and sympathizers among the German-trained army officers, such as General José Evaristo Uriburu.

Typical of the postwar change was the case of Leopoldo Lugones, one of Argentina's leading men of letters. Formerly an anarchist, after 1918 Lugones reversed his course, became a familiar figure at the capital's Military Club, and dinned into his hearers there, and his readers everywhere, such phrases as "Democracy is done for," "The universities are hot-beds of leftists," "The professional politicians are ruining the country," and as a logical conclusion, "The hour of the sword has struck," meaning, the time has come when the armed forces must intervene to save the country.

Likewise typical of the decade was the growth of group opposition outside the political parties. This included the right-wing but relatively moderate organization Argentine Catholic Action, whose exclusively spiritual mission did not prevent its organ, the weekly journal *Criterio*, from praising fascist dictators. It also included military lodges that were partly professional and partly political, a revolutionary youth group called the Republican League, and its counterpart for grown-ups, the May Legion (Legión de Mayo).

But Irigoyen helped to dig his own grave. Though now 76 years old and senile, he clung jealously to a monopoly of power. Psychopathically suspicious and secretive, he shut himself off from his own cabinet ministers. When he could not act, which was often, he would let no one act for him. When he did act he showed a perverse talent for doing the wrong thing.

Shameless abuse of power for partisan purposes characterized Irigoyen's second administration. A fair appraisal of this aspect of it was given by Ricardo Rojas, himself a Radical, in the following words, written in 1932:

> Perhaps the great sin of the Radical government has been . . . its violation of the Saenz Peña electoral law in Córdoba, in Mendoza, and in San Juan; in having nullified the collaboration of the cabinet and control within the legislature, because of a misconceived sentiment of party solidarity. . . . All this signifies forgetfulness of historic Radicalism, of its doctrine of free suffrage, and of its democratic ideals.

Yet the Argentine people have put up with worse political performances than this, and Irigoyen might not have been turned out but for the worldwide economic depression that began with the Wall Street crash in October 1929, and his do-nothing attitude in the face of its disastrous consequences in Argentina. Economic growth, and faith in its continuance, had been an essential component of the new Argentina for the previous half century. The last serious blow to it, the crash of 1890, had routed President Juárez Celman but had left the regime intact. This time, Irigoyen's inaction in the face of an even graver shock finished the regime as well as its chief.

Argentina's vulnerable economy was hit early and hard by the depression, and the Radical government's prestige and power began to crumble almost immediately. In March 1930 its ticket was swamped in a Buenos Aires election. By June of that year, even labor was reported to be in a "refractory temper," and shortly thereafter even the university students issued a manifesto calling on the citizenry to "rise up and fight against the chaotic and somber situation" created by the government. By this time, the American Embassy in Buenos Aires was reporting that the continuation in office of Irigoyen's "exceptionally dictatorial and extraordinarily inactive" government was "if not problematical, at least a serious problem." This was no exaggeration: on September 6 the government was overthrown.

In the past few years currency has been given a story to the effect that the United States had a hand in overthrowing Irigoyen: specifically, that Yankee oil interests in Argentina financed the coup to forestall the planned expropriation of some of their concessions in Argentina and the importation of cheap petroleum from Russia. Evidence to prove the charge is lacking, but even if it were demonstrated beyond the shadow of a doubt, it would be superfluous. For the fact is that Irigoyen was the victim of a completely indigenous and widely popular Argentine movement and its leaders and supporters included many who were either hostile or indifferent to the United States.

Momentous in its significance for Argentina, the coup of September 6, 1930, seemed at the time a small affair from every point of view. For one thing, while many applauded it, only a corporal's guard had a hand in it. It was planned and carried out as an army coup by only one high-ranking army officer, the General José E. Uriburu already mentioned, with the support of a mere handful of troops, mostly cadets. One of the very few regular officers who took an active part in it was an obscure 35-year-old captain named Juan Perón. The resistance to the coup was likewise microscopic. Hardly anyone rallied to the government's defense, and it took almost literally only a whiff of grapeshot to end the fighting, which was confined to the city of Buenos Aires. Finally, the ostensible purpose of the coup was limited to turning the rascals out and restoring constitutional government under an honest administration. Almost at once, however, Uriburu came forth with fascist ideas and plans for converting Argentina into a corporative state. He failed to carry them out, but ever since then attacks from various quarters on Argentina's traditional political and economic structure have continued. So also has military intervention in the government. In retrospect, therefore, September 6, 1930, looms large as a convenient marker for the beginning of a new phase—the contemporary phase —of Argentine history.

Irigoyen, who had resigned on the very eve of the coup, was imprisoned on Martin García island in the Plata River. Few mourned his fall at the time, but after his death in 1933 his rehabilitation proceeded apace. It was probably speeded by the quick disillusionment of most Argentines over the sequel to his fall.

FIVE

FLOURISH OF TRUMPETS:
ENTER THE MILITARY
1930-1943

The revolution of 1930 marks the assumption by the Argentine armed forces of the new role of decision maker in public affairs, which they were to play in various ways for the next third of a century. But that revolution also revealed a persistent flaw that has made it difficult or impossible for the military to perform their self-appointed role successfully, namely their incessant internecine discord. Due in part to personal and interservice rivalries, their schisms also reflect the fragmentation of the Argentine civilian society from which both officers and men are drawn and with which even the professionalized officer corps continues to maintain contact.

The armed forces' inability to agree among themselves on how to use their decisive power has been a major source of the instability that has characterized Argentine public life most of the time since 1930. This protracted instability, too, was something new in Argentine history; for combined duration and intensity, there had been nothing to match it in the century elapsed between the advent of the tyrant Rosas and that of dictator Uriburu. As will be shown in the next chapter, the inability of the armed forces to agree among themselves facilitated the emergence in the 1940s of still another new power group, organized labor.

The present chapter will discuss the first phase of the military's new role. This phase is delimited by two military revolts, each successful in a single day: General Uriburu's on September 6, 1930, and one on June 4, 1943, which was directed not by an individual but by a junta. In between, Argentina was ruled first, for 17 months, by a military dictator, Uriburu, who sought but failed to establish a kind of fascist system. Then, for a little more than ten years, it was governed by a revised version of the pre-1914 oligarchy, under constitutional forms but on military sufferance until the second coup turned it out in 1943 and set up another military dictatorship.

The Role of the Military and the New Nationalism

The Argentine armed forces' new political role involved a sharp break with long-established principle and almost as sharp a departure from precedent. As we have already seen, Argentina's Liberator, General José de San Martín, had established that principle, summing it up in the oft-quoted apothegm, "The army is a lion that must be kept in a cage and not let out until the day of battle." Later, this principle was incorporated in the Constitution of 1853 in a clause, still unaltered, which makes the president commander-in-chief of the nation's armed forces; and the president, elected in substantially the same manner as the president of the United States, is of course the head of the civil government.

First among the circumstances that led to a reversal of these roles was the modernization and professionalization of Argentina's armed forces, and their consequent growth in proficiency and self-esteem. Ironically, this long process was given its first major impulse by leaders such as Mitre and Sarmiento, whose purpose was to strengthen the civil government against the militarism of that day as represented by the caudillos and their gaucho hordes. Thus, it was the "schoolteacher president" Sarmiento who founded the Colegio Militar (1870) and the Escuela Naval (1872), the Argentine equivalents of West Point and Annapolis. In the next few decades, Roca, Pellegrini, and Roca's protégé General Pablo R. Riccheri carried on in the same spirit. In 1884 the General Staff was reorganized; beginning in 1899 German military missions and equipment were imported; in 1900 the Escuela Superior de Guerra (a national war college for higher officers) was founded; in 1901 compulsory military service was established; and in the next few years the character of the officer corps was profoundly altered by the forced retirement of many older officers and the adoption of seniority and technical proficiency as the criteria for promotion.

As a result of this last change, the middle class supplanted the oligarchy as the main source of the officer corps. The fact that the middle class consisted to a large extent of "new Argentines," the sons of immigrants, weakened the hold of Argentine traditions, including San Martín's principle, on the nation's professionalized, self-confident armed forces. The alienation was most pronounced in the German-trained army.

In the 1920s and '30s several other circumstances reinforced the trend. Partly by contagion from abroad, two related ideas gained wide acceptance in Argentina. One was that the political parties were corrupt and incompetent and representative democracy a failure; the other, that it was the armed forces' mission to redeem the country. Both ideas fell on fertile soil in Argentina, where they had an exceptionally long and vigorous life. That they did so was partly the fault of the civilians themselves, and the Radicals were as much to blame as their right-wing opponents. When the latter used the armed forces to overthrow Irigoyen's government in 1930, they were only giving him some of his own medicine, for he had done all he could to gain military support for the revolts of 1890, 1893, and 1905; and when in office he constantly played politics with the armed forces. His successors in the Radical leadership also tried to stir up military revolts for several years after 1930, though with no better success.

Finally, nationalism conditioned the behavior and thought of most Argentines, including the military, during this period. There were, however, different kinds of nationalism and these corresponded to, if they did not cause, divisions within the military as well as the civilians. Both of the two main types of nationalism, liberal and integral, described by general students of the subject flourished in Argentina at this time. Liberal nationalism was the older type there; except during the Rosas period, it was dominant at all times before 1930. Unfortunately for its continued preponderance, liberal nationalism became identified with the oligarchy and so with exploitation of the masses and with a foreign economic and cultural penetration that was said to be stunting the country's growth, undermining its traditional culture, and making a farce of its vaunted independence. On such grounds deep dissatisfaction with Argentina's liberal or "canonical" nationalism was voiced as early as 1910 even by genuine liberals such as Ricardo Rojas.

Spurred by the deep economic depression of the early 1930s and its sequel in Argentina, integral nationalism expressed in part a revulsion against the fruits of the liberal variety. In foreign relations it was characterized by xenophobia, aggressiveness, and chauvinism; anti-imperialism and anticolonialism were among its favorite themes. In domestic affairs its proponents held that, in order to achieve the goals of "true" independence and greatness, the Argentine nation must be integrated at whatever cost to established provincial, individual, or other freedoms. They also made an effort, however misguided, to cope with new problems of great urgency, such as the rise of a rootless proletariat, social fragmentation, and economic lag in a deteriorating international situation, at a time when the political parties were apparently unable to meet the challenge under the existing rules of the game.

The foregoing descriptions of both varieties of nationalism are comprehensive models, and there were probably not many Argentines who subscribed to either type in every detail; there was certainly a wide variety of views and behavior among those associated with each. The liberal nationalists, for example, included not only the essentially democratic and civilian Sarmiento but also General Agustín Justo. Among the integral nationalists there was an even more glaring contrast between the elitist authoritarianism of General Uriburu and the popular, majoritarian tyranny promoted by Colonel (later General) Juan Perón after 1945. In short, while nearly all Argentine groups draped themselves in the national flag, there was not the remotest approach to a general consensus on the meaning of Argentine nationalism.

Uriburu: The Failure of Elitist Nationalism

After the quick success of his coup amid general applause, General Uriburu set up a dictatorship and tried to convert Argentina into a corporative state under elite control. For one reason or another, his plan, first publicly revealed on October 1, 1930, met with overwhelming opposition among his military associates as well as the civilian population. Some disliked it most because they regarded it as an alien importation, smacking of Italian fascism; others because it would mean scrapping Argentina's traditional democratic system, to which conservatives as well as liberals had professed allegiance for generations past; and still others for more personal reasons. The last-named group included political leaders whose careers would be blighted if Uriburu succeeded in destroying the political party system; it also included General Justo's large following in the armed forces, which was a rival of the Uriburu faction. As for mass support, Uriburu made no effort to build it up until too late, and in any case it was in all probability ruled out by the elitist character of the plan; this was a sobering lesson that was not lost on one of Uriburu's junior associates, Captain Juan Perón.

Yet Uriburu did some things that won applause at the time and others that had an enduring significance. His adventure should certainly not be dismissed as a crude imitation of Mussolini, as was alleged at the time and has been repeated since. If Uriburu had a prototype, it was the Spanish dictator Primo de Rivera rather than Mussolini; which is not altogether surprising when it is recalled that Uriburu came of one of Argentina's traditional Spanish families, unmixed with the teeming Italian immigrant stock. Like Primo de Rivera, Uriburu was a provincial aristocrat, a professional soldier, and faithful, after his fashion, to the Church. His movement was made to match and, like Primo's, it had conflicting aims: to strengthen existing hierarchies and to promote industrialization.

Similarly, Uriburu's grand design for Argentina was little affected by his German military training. This may have strengthened the strain of authoritarianism in him, but no fellow countryman of Rosas or descendant of Spaniards would need help from Germans in developing this strain. Uriburu was a growth of his native soil at its most Argentine, the provincial soil, and when he did borrow from abroad he put the stamp of Argentina on the imported goods. The point needs to be stressed, for the same error has been made in interpreting other Argentine leaders, including Perón.

Aside from his ill-fated political plan, Uriburu's administration was notable for its strengthening of the military and for its economic nationalism. Despite the economic depression and a thumping deficit, he gave the army forces a larger slice of the national budget, stepped up arms imports from Europe, increased the annual quota of draftees from approximately 21,000 to 26,000, and doubled the number of cadets in the Colegio Militar, or military academy, raising it from 350 to 700.

Yet Uriburu failed to win the solid support of the military for the simple reason that he dispensed rewards and punishments on the basis of political loyalty to himself. As a result, the rival Justo faction was only stiffened in its determination to oust him. In fact, Justo planned a revolt in 1931, but this became unnecessary when Uriburu, baffled and mortally ill, permitted Justo's election to the presidency in November of that year.

Economic nationalism found expression in Uriburu's tariff and petroleum policies. Domestic manufactures, neglected even by the middle-class Radical party, were now encouraged in various ways, particularly by tariff protection. The purpose was to promote the nation's economic independence by strengthening its economy through diversification. As regards petroleum policy, Uriburu did not carry nationalism to the extreme of expropriating the foreign oil concessions—that would have seemed to rubber-stamp a Radical project of the late 1920s. He did, however, refuse to cancel Radical decrees that had denied extensive oil deposits to the foreign companies by reserving them for exploitation by the national petroleum agency, Y.P.F. Furthermore, he added to the latter's domain the whole of Argentine Tierra del Fuego, which proved to have substantial petroleum resources. Finally, he provided Y.P.F. with 10 million pesos of government funds for the construction of plants and storage facilities, and supported it in its refusal to join the foreign oil companies in raising prices.

The rock on which Uriburu foundered was political. As the only means of getting indispensable military and civilian support for his revolution, he had promised publicly to respect the constitution. This won his regime a provisional but valuable endorsement by the nation's Supreme Court, which recognized it as a *de facto* government. The court's action then enabled him to issue a constitutionally valid declaration of a state of siege suspending all guarantees of individual rights. He issued the declaration at once, and maintained and enforced it throughout his brief administration. Moreover, it was soon apparent to all that he was determined to do everything in his power to scrap the constitution in favor of his corporative system of government.

Uriburu's power was not equal to the task. The stronger Justo military faction of liberal nationalists held him to his promise to change the constitution only by constitutional means, not by decree. This threw the question back into the civilian political arena, where our bluff soldier proved himself a complete tyro. Overconfident because of the public acclaim that had greeted his September coup, and disregarding the advice of wiser heads among his associates, that time must be taken to organize and build up a popular following, he permitted a free election to be held in Buenos Aires in April 1931, only seven months after the coup. The result was a disastrous defeat for the Uriburu ticket; the worst blow to him was that the great bulk of the opposition vote went to the supposedly discredited Radicals. He cancelled the election and set to work organizing paramilitary as well as political groups, but it was too late, for his military and civilian foes only redoubled the pressure on him to restore normal constitutional government.

Too ill to hold out longer, Uriburu permitted a nation-wide election to be held in November 1931. It was won by a coalition of conservatives (now called National Democrats), Antipersonalist Radicals, and Independent Socialists, headed by General Agustín Justo. The Radical nominee for president, ex-President Alvear, who had returned to the Personalist fold, was disqualified on grounds that were at least plausible: the constitutional prohibition against a president's succeeding himself was interpreted to mean that there must be an interval of a full presidential term of six years, whereas only three years had elapsed since the end of Alvear's term. The Radicals thereupon refused to nominate anyone else, and reverted to their pre-1912 policy of abstention and revolution. But, as individuals, most of them voted in the election, casting their ballots for the opposition ticket headed by the luckless Lisandro de la Torre, able leader of a minor party, the Progressive Democrats. As a result, the combined vote for the two major tickets was almost as large as in the election of 1928 (approximately 1,100,000 and 1,200,000, respectively), and the vote was fairly evenly divided, Justo receiving 607,-000 and de la Torre 488,000. The losers cried fraud with some reason, but they were to repeat the cry with still better reason in the next decade, which hostile historians never tire of calling the "infamous decade."

Justo: Economic Recovery

Justo had a sense of history, and one of his sharpest Argentine critics couples the characterization of him as "innately Machiavellian" with the admission that it was his "noble ambition" to go down in history as one of the nation's great presidents. The trouble was, continues this writer, that Justo was so far behind the times as to take as his models two soldier-presidents of a bygone age, Bartolomé Mitre and Julio A. Roca. (The latter's son, of the same name, was in fact Justo's vice president.) And what was wrong with this? Simply, we are told, that Justo was "impregnated to the marrow of his bones" with the ideology of the old regime represented by Mitre and Roca, "the first dogma of which consisted in veneration for foreign capital."

There is some truth in this criticism, but even as a brief appraisal of Justo's administration it omits several equally important items from both sides of the ledger; it also gives the misleading impression that Justo merely continued, or revived, the old regime. On the credit side it should be added that he expedited Argentina's recovery from an exceptionally deep economic depression; launched, and to a large extent carried out, the country's first really nationwide highway construction program; promoted the growth of the domestic economy by fiscal reforms, and made an honest though unavailing effort to restore the principle and practice of nonintervention by the military in politics. Also, while his administration did little to promote it, a substantial growth of domestic manufactures began at this time, with highly important political and demographic as well as economic results.

On the debit side, Justo aided in reviving the old regime's system of limited democracy. In his administration, one half or more of the people were excluded from voting, by fraud, intimidation, or otherwise, and the national election in 1937, his last year in office, was by all accounts one of the most fraudulent in Argentine history. Also on the debit side was his administration's neglect of the masses in favor of the classes. Its failures in the field of social legislation and labor relations were all the more striking because of the rapid growth of the urban proletariat and because of the advances in social legislation which were being made by the middle 1930s in neighboring countries—Uruguay, Chile, and even Brazil—not to mention remoter lands, such as Colombia, Mexico, and the United States. And hard times were no excuse, for by 1936 the depression was a thing of the past in Argentina and the national economy was booming again.

While it is true that Justo brought about a restoration of important features of the old conservative regime, his differed from it in two major respects. In the first place, the conservative party, which now took the name National Democrat, no longer had a monopoly of power such as the National Autonomous Party had enjoyed for a third of a century after 1880. The new situation was symbolized by the election of 1931, in which the National Democrats won by allying themselves with the Antipersonalist Radicals but had to be content with second place on the national ticket, while first place went to the Antipersonalist Justo. The alliance, made permanent under the name of Concordancia, ruled Argentina until 1943, but in the only other presidential election of this period, in 1937, the National Democrats again had to settle for second place, with an Antipersonalist again in first place. Also, Justo lost no love on his National Democrat allies and found little room for them in his cabinet; on the other hand, one of the most important posts in it, that of Minister of Economy, went to an Independent Socialist, Federico Pinedo.

In the second place, Justo's administration differed from the old regime in policy as well. There were, to be sure, some important resemblances. Several of his measures greatly benefited not only "foreign capitalism" but also its domestic ally, the oligarchy, including the estancieros and related business, banking, and professional groups. The net result was to prop up the old pre-1912 type of economy based on foreign trade and investments, with Great Britain as the principal trading partner and investor. At the same time, however, Justo made some important new departures, mainly in the direction of establishing national control of the economy. His measures of this kind resembled those being taken in many parts of the Atlantic World under the impact of the Great Depression. In Argentine experience, however, they accorded more closely with policies of the Radical and Uriburu periods since 1916 than with those of the oligarchical regime before that date.

Most of Justo's chief economic measures had been taken by 1935, after which the administration's pristine vigor and inventiveness declined. Two of the first and most important measures reinforced Argentina's special ties with Great Britain. Both were taken on Argentine initiative. First, in September 1932, an expert from the Bank of England was brought to Argentina to study its banking and financial system and recommend reforms; with some modifications, his report was followed in setting up, two years later, a key institution, the Banco Central Argentino, privately owned by foreigners as well as Argentines but operated under government supervision, which centralized control of currency, commercial credit, and foreign exchange. Then, in February 1933 Vice President Roca was sent to England to negotiate a treaty which would protect Argentine beef against the threatened loss of the British market as a consequence of the adoption of the Imperial Preference system at the Ottawa conference in 1932. The British, represented by Walter Runciman, President of the Board of Trade, played hard to get, but Argentine concessions finally led to the signing of the Roca-Runciman agreement in May 1933.

While both measures exposed Justo to the charge of *vendepatria*, the critics' main target was the Roca-Runciman pact. All Argentina got out of the pact was Britain's commitment not to reduce its purchases of Argentine chilled beef below the level reached a year earlier (the spring quarter of 1932). Even this promise was subject to the qualification that Britain might reduce the volume of such purchases, if in its judgment this was necessary in order to maintain a remunerative price level for producers in the United Kingdom (England's prime beef came from Scotland; Argentine chilled beef was for its middle class). Britain's gains were many. Argentina agreed to retain only 15 per cent of the meat export business for its nationals' *frigoríficos*, and to give the remaining 85 per cent to those owned by foreigners; these included American as well as British firms, but Britain was given control of the export licenses. Argentina also agreed to reserve her sterling balance for the service of debts to Britain, to reduce her tariffs on British goods to the levels of 1930, and to leave British coal on the free list. The last item was important because British coal was the chief source of power in Argentina at that time. Finally, by a protocol to the Roca-Runciman pact, Argentina promised to accord "benevolent treatment" to "British capital in the public services and other enterprises."

The pact and its protocol provoked a storm of protest in Argentina and fanned the spreading flames of nationalism. The flames leaped still higher when in 1935 the Argentine government accorded "benevolent treatment" to British tramway interests in Buenos Aires at the expense of local owners of free-lance *colectivos*—a kind of combination taxi-cab and microbus. The hostile reaction in Argentina is understandable, but so also is Justo's decision to enter into the pact. Argentina was still in the trough of the economic depression and the new British imperial preference system contained a real threat of further injury to the Argentine economy, in much the same way that the European Common Market was to threaten the economies of several Latin American countries a generation later. Argentina had to export or die, for more than one fourth of its national income was derived from foreign trade. Something must be done quickly, for meat exports to Britain amounted to 16 per cent of Argentina's total exports. If the protection of these was directly beneficial to only a few, those few were so essential to the welfare of the national economy that most Argentines shared indirectly in the benefits. It is easy to say that Roca, and Justo above him, should have been harder bargainers and should, for instance, have threatened the British with reprisals against their extensive holdings in Argentina, but the David-and-Goliath pattern has always had more admirers than imitators. Finally, there was no other way in which Justo could have met the emergency. He had no time to develop alternative markets for Argentine meat. The United States might have seemed a good prospect because it had by this time become the chief source of Argentine imports, but even before the depression the United States had eliminated itself by a sanitary regulation (1927) barring beef imports from Argentina on the ground that Argentine cattle were infected with the hoof-and-mouth disease.

Justo gave Argentina its first income tax and its first comprehensive program of road building. Both measures had been planned by Uriburu. The income tax was imposed less on grounds of social justice than as a fiscal device rendered necessary by deficits inherited from previous administrations and by the catastrophic decline, result-

ing from the depression, of customs revenues, which had always hitherto been the government's principal source of revenue. The road
building program is one answer to the charge that Justo was sub-
servient to the British, for spokesmen of the British-owned railways,
which represented two thirds of all British investments in Argentina,
stoutly opposed the program on the ground that the new highways
created unfair government-supported competition with the railways.

In some respects Justo's economic policy was marked by a mild
but unmistakable spirit of nationalism. Internal taxes on consumption were centralized and standardized—a measure which Finance
Minister Pinedo described as completing the economic unification of
Argentina, since it put an end to the use of such taxes by provincial
and municipal governments to create what amounted to internal customs barriers to trade. Justo also gave strong support to the government oil agency, Y.P.F., which was now well on its way to becoming
the chief symbol of Argentine economic nationalism. Still other
measures signalized Argentina's first substantial shift from free enterprise to government direction of the economy. These included the
establishment of four juntas or boards, one each for meat, cereals,
milk and milk products, and the wine industry, including viticulture.
While the functions of these boards differed somewhat in each case,
all of them were given broad control of commercial operations, with
special attention to prices. Ample precedent was thus provided for
the much more extensive government controls over the economy
established by Perón in the next decade.

On the other side of the ledger was the Port of Rosario scandal
arising from Minister Pinedo's renegotiation of a contract with a
French company which since the start of the century had made fabulous profits from the construction of Rosario's modern port and its
operation. By the new contract, it was charged, the government further enriched the company under conditions that indicated at least
waste and favoritism, if not corruption. Pinedo defended the contract
stoutly, both then and later, but many were not convinced and the
pros and cons of the affair, which was highly complicated, are still
debatable. At the time, it was significant mainly because of the opposition's success in exploiting it as additional evidence of the regime's
corrupt alliance with foreign capitalism.

Decline of the Parties

On these and other grounds extreme nationalists of both the left and the right attacked the regime with increasing vigor throughout Justo's administration. The storm did not break until after his retirement and the beginning of World War II in 1939, but it was already gathering. In the atmosphere of growing national and international tension, many Argentines regarded his liberal brand of nationalism as at best outdated. In addition, the decay of the opposition parties became so obvious, and the regime's electoral frauds closed the door to peaceful change so firmly, that public confidence in the country's democratic system was shaken. Clearly, the situation was shaping up for another military coup, despite Justo's efforts to keep his companions-in-arms out of politics.

As evidence of his good intentions in this respect, Justo chose as his first ministers of War and Navy two of the officers least involved in the military's political conspiracies and other activities. One of them, the Minister of War, had just given striking proof of his loyalty to the San Martín tradition of a nonpolitical army. On July 10, 1931, in the midst of Uriburu's military dictatorship, he had delivered a speech, in his capacity as head of the Círculo Militar (the army officers' club in Buenos Aires), on "The Mission of the Army," in which he told his fellow officers plainly that "the army is not a political force . . . but a child of the people . . . at the service of the nation . . . [and] is guided by the old spirit of the Army of the Andes," meaning the army commanded by San Martín.

Yet many of the officers remained of another mind—or rather, of other minds, for even those who agreed that the armed forces did have a political mission disagreed violently with one another on the nature and purpose of the mission. Some joined in revolutionary conspiracies hatched by the Radicals between 1932 and 1935; others responded to the growing attraction of fascism, Nazism, and Spanish Falangism; and still others adhered to older Argentine varieties of authoritarianism. The second and third groups gained added impetus when the Radicals abandoned "abstention and revolution" in 1935 and resumed normal political activity. Radicalism soon took on the appearance of the wave of the future, and that was a wave which these officers were even less disposed to tolerate now than in the later days of Irigoyen.

As the presidential election of 1937 approached, the rising Radical tide made Justo himself uneasy over the chances of passing control to the right people. Accordingly, he and his followers simply stole the election by fraud and force (the force of the local police, not of the army, which was kept in its barracks). The Concordancia ticket, headed by his hand-picked presidential candidate and fellow Anti-personalist, Roberto M. Ortiz, won by a comfortable margin.

Yet, except in the narrowest partisan sense the Concordancia's victory was pyrrhic. It damaged Justo's own reputation beyond repair by making a mockery of his vaunted restoration of normal constitutional government. In this respect, at least, he did reproduce the practices of the old oligarchical regime. For the political health of the nation, the effect was disastrous. Coming on top of all that had gone before, it seemed to confirm what nonconformists had been saying for years past: that in Argentina democracy was only a snare to facilitate the domination and exploitation of the nation at large by a privileged few.

To make the crisis of political confidence still worse, the Radicals, the only large opposition party, were in disarray. This may seem to contradict the statement, made above, that the Radical label recovered its charm as the 1930s wore on, but that statement should be set beside another: that the party suffered increasingly from a famine of leadership. The fact is that what won respect was the label, not the leaders. This was not because there were no able men among the Radicals; some of them had every talent except the indispensable one of winning nationwide support among his fellows. Alvear, who came closest to being a truly national leader, never succeeded in healing the breach between the party's Antipersonalist and Irigoyenist wings. In a sense he reopened it by abandoning "abstention and revolution" and returning the party to participation in elections, for many left-wing Radicals protested that this amounted only to validating a fraudulent regime that would never let itself be voted out of office. One result was the formation of a small but vigorous dissident group, called FORJA, which produced Argentina's first comprehensive program of popular nationalism. This was only one of many centrifugal forces at work in the Radical party, which had become little more than a loose federation of personal and local factions.

As in the 1920s, the explanation is to be found mainly in two factors: the disruptive force of personalism, which afflicted all Argentine parties, and the disunity of the middle class, which strongly affected only the Radical party since its main strength lay in that class. By the late 1930s the second factor had become even more important than it was a decade or two earlier, for although the middle class was now larger than ever, numbering 40 per cent of the total population, it had also become more divided. To all its earlier divisions, another of considerable importance had been added by the growth of manufacturing since 1929. This produced an industrial middle sector which differed from the older commercial and professional middle sectors not only in composition and general outlook but on specific questions of public policy, and the growth of nationalism in the 1930s accentuated the difference. Generally speaking, the older commercial-professional sector favored the traditional "liberal" economic policy based on Argentine agriculture and foreign investments; directly or indirectly, they made their living from the system that had grown up under it. Those in the industrial sector, on the other hand, were more nationalistic, attacked foreign enterprise when it conflicted with their own, and clamored for tariff protection of manufactures, which was anathema to the older group.

Alvear, despite his wealth and high social standing, represented this older middle-class group politically; it was, indeed, the backbone of his political following. As a representative of the new industrial sector we may take an Italian immigrant of the early twentieth century, Torcuato di Tella, who—precisely because he apparently avoided political commitments—symbolizes the growing diversity of Argentina's so-called middle class. In the 1920s and '30s he built up a thriving business as manufacturer of assorted items, including household refrigerators, dough-mixing machines for bakers, and oil pipe and gasoline pumps for Y.P.F. All the members of his family firm were Italians; as it grew, his engineers and skilled workers were recruited from Italy; he was not even naturalized until the late 1930s. Yet this uncommitted entrepreneur did not hesitate to exploit Argentine nationalism in his advertising. As the firm's historians have written, it "continually called attention to itself as a strictly Argentine enterprise," implicitly contrasting itself with the British and other foreign-controlled interests that had long dominated Argentina and much of its industry. It also worked the vein of creole tradition; thus, in 1934 one of its advertisements showed a gaucho woman with one of the firm's refrigerators, under the caption, "Argentine . . . and with great honor." Here was a new kind of middle-class nationalism that was worse than useless to Radicals of either Irigoyen's or Alvear's kind, for it could coexist peacefully with any regime that was good for business.

Negative Diplomacy

Argentina's diplomacy under Justo was rather negative, but its international role was played with a distinction befitting the country that stood first in Latin America culturally, commercially, and in almost every other respect save size, in which it ranked third. Its role was reflected in that of its foreign minister, Carlos Saavedra Lamas, who won personal distinction on the world stage as well as in Western Hemisphere affairs. In his *annus mirabilis*, 1936, he was both awarded the Nobel Peace Prize and elected President of the League of Nations Assembly. In December of that same year he came close to dominating the important Inter-American Conference on Peace and Security, in his home city, to the discomfiture of Secretary of State Cordell Hull, head of the U.S. delegation, whose plans he frustrated. Saavedra Lamas' influence had been equally decisive at the Inter-American Conference of 1933 in Montevideo, where, after striking a bargain with Hull, he made it possible for the latter to emerge with laurels.

Why, then, was Argentine diplomacy in this period negative, and in what sense? The fault lay partly in Saavedra Lamas and partly in circumstances beyond his control. Sumner Welles, himself an expert who knew most of the leading diplomats of that era, called Saavedra Lamas one of the ablest of them all. As a technician he may well have merited the tribute, but policy was another matter. His foreign policy was a reflection of the Justo regime as refracted through his own personality. Scion of one of the country's leading patrician families and son-in-law of a former president, Roque Saenz Peña, he was a man of broad culture but excessive veneration for the law, in which he had been trained, and for the Argentine traditions in which he had been steeped; his mind was precise, legalistic, and backward looking. He would have been an ideal foreign minister in the *belle époque* before 1914, but it was his misfortune to serve in a time of troubles and catastrophic worldwide change.

Continuing an Argentine tradition, which his father-in-law had helped to fortify and which accorded with the general orientation of the Justo regime, Saavedra Lamas adopted a policy of universalism, close cooperation with the League of Nations, and special ties with Europe. Unfortunately for him, at this very time world order was breaking down, the League of Nations was headed for an early demise, and the European nations were on the point of blowing one another to bits. Conversely, he resisted the trend toward inter-American cooperation just when that was beginning a rapid growth. His resistance was aimed primarily at its chief promoter, the United States; an instance is his frustration of Hull at the 1936 conference. In this respect, too, he was following in the footsteps of his august father-in-law, whose philippic against Secretary Blaine's customs union proposal had been a highlight of a Pan American conference in 1890.

The merits of Saavedra Lamas' stand are arguable but cannot be argued here, and the point to be made is that it was essentially negative: his chief contribution, if it can be called that, was in establishing the inter-American rule of nonintervention. On the positive side, he is best remembered for the unrealistic and superfluous peace pact that bears his name; it was by supporting this and the nonintervention rule that Hull won the Argentine minister's fleeting cooperation at the Inter-American Conference of 1933. The latter's policy was often nationalist as well as negative, as in his obstruction of the efforts of other powers, including the United States, to end Bolivia's bloody Chaco War with Paraguay, in which Argentina had special interests. Likewise, in 1937, when the United States sought to promote Hemisphere defense by leasing some destroyers to Brazil, he checked the transaction by publicly protesting that it would upset the balance of power in South America to Argentina's detriment. All told, as an architect of Argentine foreign policy in this stage of the world's history, Saavedra Lamas was more ornamental than useful. At the end of the administration, in 1938, he left his country unprepared to play a positive role during World War II, which broke out the next year. As a result, a policy vacuum was created which military and other nationalists in Argentina rushed to fill.

Disintegration of the Regime

When the new president, Roberto M. Ortiz, took office in 1938, there was widespread hope that the promise to restore honestly-administered constitutional government would at last be carried out. Although elected as the Concordancia's candidate, Ortiz belonged to its relatively liberal Antipersonalist Radical wing and was reputed to be a man of complete personal integrity and also to have a talent for leadership demonstrated both in public affairs and in his private practice as a lawyer. The very fact that his education had been notoriously fraudulent gave ground for hoping that such a man would try to make amends by purifying the political process even at the expense of his own class, as Saenz Peña had done by his electoral reform law of 1912.

That is just what Ortiz did, but the war in Europe soon distracted him, then diabetes crippled him, and his well-intentioned but limited efforts at reform did less to improve the political tone than to weaken the regime by sowing dissension in the government party, especially in its National Democratic wing. As that was the wing to which Vice President Ramón S. Castillo belonged, there was a virtual change of administration when illness forced Ortiz to turn over his powers to Castillo in July 1940. The arrangement was intended to be only temporary, but, except for a brief period when Ortiz resumed his functions, the presidential powers remained in Castillo's hands until the government was overthrown in June 1943. Castillo was acting president until Ortiz resigned in June 1942 (he died in July), and president thereafter.

The policy change was greater in foreign than in domestic affairs, though the ideological conflict on both fronts tended to merge the two. Ortiz, pro-democratic and a lawyer for British interests, was neutral but benevolent toward England and France when war broke out. And both before and after that his administration took a somewhat friendlier attitude toward inter-American cooperation and the United States than Saavedra Lamas had maintained. But illness eliminated him in July 1940 just as Hitler's conquest of France and most of Western Europe opened a crucial period of decision for the American nations.

In the next eighteen months the United States moved away from neutrality, through "all aid short of war" to Britain and the other enemies of the Axis (including, after June 1941, the Soviet Union), to entry into the war after the attack on Pearl Harbor. On the other hand, Argentina, with Castillo at the helm most of the time, moved in the opposite direction, first hardening its neutrality and then giving signs of benevolence toward the Axis. Its course is understandable, if not praiseworthy. The Axis was at the height of its power; Generalissimo Franco had won the Spanish Civil War with its aid; and the Argentines had heard reports, since confirmed, that the United States did not plan to defend South America south of the northern "bulge" of Brazil, so that Argentina would be left alone to face an attack or reprisals from Hitler. And the Argentine military, whose voice was now loud again in public affairs, fully expected him to win.

Accordingly, when Castillo responded to the Pearl Harbor attack by declaring a state of siege, the measure had no anti-Axis connotation whatever and was merely designed to cripple the domestic opposition. His last major foreign policy decision reached the public a month later, January 1942, at a meeting of American foreign ministers in Rio de Janeiro. There the Argentine delegation successfully resisted heavy pressure from the United States and its Latin American friends for a resolution requiring all the American states to break relations with the Axis. Instead, the resolution only recommended a break, and that was the end of the matter so far as Castillo's government was concerned: it simply ignored the recommendation.

Castillo acted as he did because, beset by his domestic foes, he was fighting for his political life and, however misguidedly, for that of the regime. He needed all the help he could get from the state of siege and from every other available source. Ominous rumors were circulating of new military conspiracies and of communist infiltration of the now divided labor movement. The opposition parties could hardly help Castillo, even if they would; the only two of any consequence, Radical and Socialist, were suffering from a kind of bureaucratic dry rot and had lost the confidence of the people. His own party was crippled by dissension both between its National Democratic and Antipersonalist wings, and also within each wing.

In an effort to kill two birds—one political, the other military—with one stone, he gave the now key cabinet post of Minister of War to one of the Antipersonalist Justo's military associates. In order to placate the extreme nationalists among the military, who were enraged at seeing Brazil's armed force move ahead of Argentina with Lend-Lease aid from the United States, Castillo even tried secretly to obtain arms from the Axis. He failed, however, and in November 1942 his military critics forced him to replace the recently appointed Minister of War with one of their own group, General Pedro Ramírez. That was the beginning of the end for Castillo. He might perhaps have been saved by General Justo, but Justo died in January 1943.

Since Argentina's democratic tradition is as old as the nation itself and still had strong supporters in various political and social sectors at this time, it may be wondered why they did not join forces to meet this crisis. Such an effort, at first promising, was indeed made. It had its origin in a group organized in June 1940, under the name Argentine Action, to support the cause of Britain and its allies. The group was therefore pro-democratic as well as anti-Axis. Its initial focus was on foreign, not domestic affairs, but as the domestic crisis deepened, some of its leaders tried to convert it into an inter-party coalition for the defense of democracy in Argentina.

Despite the known imminence of the threat of subversion, this effort at democratic defense failed. The chief reason seems to have been that most of the leaders of the largest party, the Personalist Radicals, refused to join the coalition because they were determined to keep a free hand in the hope of winning the election in November 1943 with a ticket headed by an army general. Their candidate was to be no less a person than Castillo's new Minister of War, Pedro Ramírez, with whom they held secret conclaves in the spring of that year.

Before the Argentine Action group dissolved, it adopted a program that linked two increasingly important themes in Argentine public life: nationalism and the need for economic and social reform. When the coup took place, one of the first measures of the new military junta was to proscribe Argentine Action as pro-communist. Yet Juan Perón, who emerged from that military junta as the master of Argentina, developed a widely popular program remarkably like that of the proscribed group: a program of social justice, land reform, development of mineral resources, industrialization, and economic independence. Even his most familiar slogan, the "Third Position," was anticipated by Argentine Action's call for an "intermediate" position between free enterprise and a regimented economy. This democratic group was in step with the times, but it could not arouse like-minded civilians to concerted action and it had the military leaders against it.

The coup took place on June 4, 1943. It was exclusively the work of the military and was directed by a secret junta of generals and colonels called the G.O.U.* With little fighting and amidst a mixture of public applause and indifference, the G.O.U. gained control of the government immediately. Promising to respect the constitution, the new government was promptly accorded *de facto* recognition by the Supreme Court. Except that there was less civilian enthusiasm for the coup, it seemed to be 1930 all over again. But there was an important difference: this time there was no General Uriburu, no single commander, but a sprawling junta composed of top and middle brass, and all scrambling for power. Out of this struggle emerged a regime which, it is safe to say, was quite different from anything planned by the military conspirators.

* The letters are generally said to stand for "Grupo de Oficiales Unidos," though there are variants, including "Grupo Obra de Unificación" and "Gobierno, Orden, Unión."

SIX

ENTER THE MASSES:

PERÓN'S NEO-FASCIST NATIONALISM

1943-1946

Military dictatorship was the first result of the G.O.U.'s successful revolt of June 4, 1943. Soon, however, civilian elements were added as the struggle for power within this group developed. First came right-wing Catholic nationalists who briefly gave the regime its tone in the latter part of 1943. Later, the adoption of an industrialization plan attracted substantial support from businessmen. Most important of all, however, were the *descamisados*,* the proletarian lump who now for the first time became an effective force in Argentine public life. They did so through their organization into regimented labor unions by Colonel Juan Perón, a member of the G.O.U. Their support enabled him to win through to the presidency in 1946. Thereafter, the regimented descamisados formed one of the two main pillars of Perón's regime; the other was the armed forces.

The new regime combined the masses with the military, and authoritarianism with democracy, in a way that was new not only in Argentina but in Latin America at large. Since the pattern has subsequently become a familiar one, special interest attaches to the way in which it was established in Argentina between 1943 and 1946, as will be related in this chapter.

* "Shirtless ones," roughly the equivalent (as Perón noted) of *sansculottes* in the French Revolution.

Neo-Fascism and the New Masses

Perón produced a new kind of Latin American revolution not only by marrying the masses with the military but also by developing a new kind of fascism. In some important respects, and most of all in its intense nationalism, his brand resembled the contemporary varieties in Mussolini's Italy, Franco's Spain, and Hitler's Germany, from all of which he borrowed. But the differences were at least equally important. The European systems were based on an appeal to the middle class against the proletariat, Perón's on one to the proletariat itself. They beat down organized labor, whereas he built it up and contrived to give the newly organized workers for the first time an illusion of freedom and a sense of dignity as first-class citizens. The Europeans came much closer than Perón to achieving the totalitarian ideal, and in fact he never made a sustained, unqualified effort to impose it. Finally, while they rejected the whole apparatus of constitutional government, Perón paid constant lip service to Argentina's Constitution of 1853, followed its prescriptions in amending it, maintained the established forms of representative government and free elections, and proclaimed himself the spiritual heir of San Martín and the restorer of Argentina's primitive, true democracy after generations of oligarchical misrule. In short, Perón's fascist system was neither a carbon copy nor a composite of those in Europe, and his was more deeply rooted in his country's history than were Mussolini's, Hitler's, or Franco's in theirs.

Some of the features of Perón's regime also resembled those found in other underdeveloped countries of both hemispheres in recent years; Nasser's Egypt offers perhaps the closest parallel. Indeed, to the general student, Perón's case may be interesting mainly because it was an early example of the trend toward popular authoritarian nationalism in such countries. Yet each country puts its own individual stamp on movements of this kind, and Argentina, proud of its traditions, conscious of its uniqueness, and imbued with a sense of destiny, was certainly no exception. Moreover, when Perón came to power, Argentina was already well on its way out of the category of underdeveloped nations and into the intermediate stage. Large parts of the interior were still underdeveloped, but industrialization had recently advanced to the point that manufactures exceeded agriculture in value of product, the urban population outnumbered the rural three to one, and greater Buenos Aires, the largest urban concentration in the Western Hemisphere except New York, was also one of the greatest concentrations of maladjusted, resentful, class-conscious workers. And once again Buenos Aires was to play the key role.

In the decade preceding Perón's rise the character of the porteño labor force had changed sharply, with political consequences that seem clear though they cannot be documented. Between 1934 and 1943 industrial output nearly doubled, and with it the number of industrial workers. Even more important was the displacement of immigrants from abroad by migrants from the Argentine interior as the principal element in this labor force. In 1914 foreign immigrants still made up, as they had done for the past generation, one half the total population of the Greater Buenos Aires area (and a still larger proportion of its labor force), but by 1947 the figure had been cut to barely more than one fourth. The decline was most rapid between 1936 (36 per cent) and 1947 (26 per cent). These eleven years were also the period of most rapid growth of internal migration, and the increase was sudden as well as extraordinarily rapid. After inching forward from 11 per cent in 1914 to 12 per cent twenty-two years later, the proportion of internal migrants in the population of Greater Buenos Aires nearly trebled in the next eleven years, reaching 29 per cent in 1947. Now for the first time in history foreign immigrants were outnumbered in Buenos Aires by Argentina's own migrants from the back country.

Chief among the many factors contributing to the reversal was the economic depression after 1929. This halted immigration temporarily (as depressions had always done in Argentina) and, together with growing nationalism, led to restrictions on immigration that stunted its revival after the depression passed. The depression also, directly or indirectly, threw many rural workers in the back country out of jobs and then provided them with new jobs in urban areas, above all Buenos Aires, by the stimulus it gave to the growth of domestic industry. By 1936 some 83,000 of these internal migrants were being added to the metropolitan area's population each year, and in the next decade the annual average grew to 96,000.

This large, sustained, and novel accretion from the back country could not fail to make its mark even on so populous a city as Greater Buenos Aires, which had 3.4 million inhabitants in 1936 and 4.7 million in 1947. The political function and influence of these new-comers needs further study, but there seems to be no question that they rallied behind Perón almost to a man and were a major source of his popular support in this key city, in which the fate of the whole nation had been settled in every revolutionary crisis since 1890. These displaced persons were not only poor and resentful; coming from the interior, where the Indian strain had been strong in colonial and early national times, they were also so swarthy that most of the older porteños referred to them contemptuously as *negritos* and *cabecitas negras*, whereas Perón welcomed them with open arms to the ranks of his "dear descamisados." Also, unless their behavior differed widely from that of other native Argentines, they were far more politically active from the start than the immigrant stock who had formerly preponderated in Greater Buenos Aires.* And if, on the other hand, they needed to be activated politically, Perón and his henchmen soon saw to that. Finally, all the existing political parties, including the Socialists and Radicals, had not only fallen into general discredit but had in particular lost contact with the masses. All of them had also lost whatever talent they may once have had for coping with new situations, and the situation that now confronted them was profoundly revolutionary.

In short, a political vacuum existed. This situation seemed made to order for such a leader as Perón, and for several years he exploited it with complete success.

From Military Coup to Revolution

When the G.O.U. seized power on June 4, 1943, all its members seem to have agreed on one aim: a great strengthening of the nation's armed forces and its power position in South America, especially in order to meet the new challenge from the reanimated and rearming Brazil of Getulio Vargas. The G.O.U. members were also

---

* In all six presidential elections from 1910 to 1958 the proportion of native-born Argentines who voted far exceeded the proportion of voters to total population (i.e., native-born plus immigrant). For example, the respective percentages were 77 and 41 in 1928, and 84 and 56 in 1946.

unanimous in one assumption: that the armed forces must be the final arbiter of questions of public policy in Argentina, with power to carry out a corrective intervention when, in their judgment, the civil government failed to function properly.

In other respects, however, there was disagreement among the members of the group as to the use they should make of the power they had seized, and underlying this disagreement was the personal struggle for individual pre-eminence. One major issue was whether they should take the quickest road to rearmament by cooperating with the United States in the war effort and obtaining a share of Lend-Lease aid, as Brazil was already doing to its great advantage. This course promised not only the quickest but the only early solution of the G.O.U.'s major problem, rearmament. Yet most of the group opposed it, whether because of sympathy with the Axis or belief that the Axis was sure to win the war (this belief persisted in the highest ranks of the army as late as June 1944), or because of attachment to neutrality as a traditional national policy, or, to paraphrase John Quincy Adams, from the determination not to let Argentina become a cockboat in the wake of the American man-of-war.

Two manifestoes were issued by the G.O.U. at an early date, but in view of its internal disagreements from the start, neither of these can be taken as representing the unanimous opinion of the group on its objectives. The first was a secret manifesto, circulated only among the armed services some three weeks before the coup. This exuded nationalism, militarism, fascism, and sympathy for the Axis. The other, a public manifesto issued just after the coup, was of a totally different tenor, promising respect for the Constitution, early elections, and loyal inter-American cooperation. By these promises the Provisional Government obtained prompt *de facto* recognition from the Supreme Court—following the precedent set by the court at the time of Uriburu's revolt in 1930. Such recognition was no empty gesture, for it contributed greatly to the smooth establishment of the regime's authority over a people who, if not law-abiding, were so law-conscious that Argentina was known as "a nation of *abogados* (lawyers)."

Within a week after General Ramírez took office, the military dictatorship began to break its promises of constitutionality, republicanism, early and free elections, and fulfillment of international obligations, including those that committed Argentina to inter-American cooperation. Yet it would be a great mistake to regard the military dictatorship of 1943-45 as simply a fulfillment of the military-fascist blueprint contained in the G.O.U.'s secret manifesto of May 1943. In fact, the character of the regime underwent two substantial changes during this period, first through its brief identification with right-wing Catholic nationalism, and then through the enduring merger of its militarism with the left-wing popular nationalism of Perón's descamisados. Moreover, as it moved from the first to the second of these stages, there was also a change in its military leadership, for in March 1944 the G.O.U., in which socially conservative officers of the highest rank were influential if not dominant, was dissolved and supplanted by the more homogeneous and radical "Colonels' clique," a kind of Young Turks group headed by Perón. His friend General Edelmiro Farrell supplanted Ramírez as President and he himself soon became Minister of War and Vice President.

The G.O.U.'s brief honeymoon with right-wing Catholics in the latter half of 1943 was a trial marriage that failed. Yet it calls for comment here because of the reasons both for the trial and for its failure, and because the right-wing Catholics continued to play an important role, especially in the 1950s. Apparently, the trial was made because the politically inexperienced military rulers soon felt the need of civilian aid in running the government. Given the character of the G.O.U., the choice of right-wing Catholic nationalists for this role was a natural one. Among them were Carlos Ibarguren, who had been one of Uriburu's chief advisers in 1930-1931, and Gustavo Martínez Zuviría, best known as a novelist writing under the pen-name "Hugo Wast." The Catholic nationalists were used primarily to promote the regime's program of thought control. They made Catholic instruction in the schools compulsory and began the purge of the universities which was to continue at an uneven pace until Perón completed it a few years later.

Reduced to its simplest terms, the answer to the question why the G.O.U.'s honeymoon with these right-wing civilians came to an end so soon is that there was no future for the regime in continuing to identify itself with the right-wing elite, as Uriburu had done. Its best chance of survival lay in shifting to the alliance with the masses prescribed by Perón. Yet his prescription was so bitter a dose for many of his fellow officers that he finally succeeded in making them swallow it only after a hard fight lasting some eighteen months and climaxed by a near-outbreak of civil war in October 1945.

Perón and Eva

Perón's views in this critical period were doubtless shaped in some degree by his middle-class origin and early years in a German-trained army. More immediate determinants were his experience as a supporter of Uriburu in the frustrated revolution of 1930-31 and his observations in Italy and Spain on a military mission in 1939-41. He was born on October 8, 1895, in a provincial Buenos Aires town, of parents who represented the two principal strains in the Argentine people: his father the Italian, his mother the Spanish creole. Both sides of the family were middle class and neither was a newcomer to Argentina; in fact, Perón's paternal grandfather had been a successful physician in the city of Buenos Aires. Whether from bad luck or bad management, however, Juan's father met with no success in a migratory life that took him from the banks of the Plata to sheep-raising Patagonia and back again to a small country town in the Province of Buenos Aires.

Young Juan thus grew up in an atmosphere of insecurity on the fringe of the rural middle class, sharing the resentment against the established order that runs through the pseudo-gaucho poem *Martín Fierro*, of which he later claimed to have been an avid reader in his youth and which he certainly cited time and again in his public addresses after 1943. Yet along with nostalgia for the lawless gaucho days he combined, as did other members of Argentina's increasingly unstable and amorphous middle class, an affinity for the discipline and order of the German-trained army. That was the career young Perón chose. The choice was all the easier for him since an uncle and a cousin of his were already officers in the army. In 1911 he entered the Colegio Militar. Nineteen years later, at the age of thirty-five, he was still only a captain; promotion was not rapid in those days.

In that same year came Perón's experience as a participant in Uriburu's abortive revolution. As a result, he understood better than most that permanent identification with right-wing Catholicism and elitist ideas would be a permanent bar to the broad popular support the regime must win if it was to survive in the kind of society that existed in Argentina. The country's only previous dictatorship, that of Rosas, the patron saint to many in Perón's coterie, had succeeded in combining Catholic conservatism and nationalism with popular support provided by gauchos and urban workers. But times had changed, the gauchos had disappeared, immigration and industrialization had transformed and vastly enlarged the urban populace, and at least in the cities the Catholic Church no longer counted for much with the masses. A new formula was needed.

Whatever other sources Perón may have used in meeting this need, he probably drew heavily upon his observations in Europe, where he spent most of 1939 and 1940. His observations were not those of the ordinary military man or tourist. His mental qualities were far above the average. They were of course displayed first and foremost in his own professional field. He taught for five years in the 1930s in his country's National War College and was the author of several books and articles on military subjects. But his interests were broader, including social studies, philosophy, and history, and he was not unduly modest about discussing them publicly. In 1937, for instance, he submitted a paper to a gathering of professional historians, the Second International Congress of the History of America, held at Buenos Aires; not surprisingly, his paper dealt with San Martín's crossing of the Andes in 1817. Years later he read a paper to a congress of philosophers, and he conducted a newspaper column under the pen-name *Descartes*. He was anything but a deep or systematic thinker and his mind was more like a sponge, but it was a top-quality sponge, and he made such good use of it that all those who knew him were impressed by the range of his knowledge as well as by the extraordinary retentiveness of his memory. By the time he returned from Europe, if not earlier, he had widened his sources by learning English, French, and Italian.

Perón's stay in Europe included visits to France, Germany, Hungary, and Albania, but, except perhaps in strictly military matters, none of these impressed him so much as did his long residence in Italy and his brief passage through Spain, still prostrate from its civil war of 1936-39. His alleged statement that "I will do what Mussolini did, but without his mistakes," represents his attitude with fidelity. And what were Mussolini's mistakes that Perón must avoid? One must have been alliance with a greater power, Germany, that dragged Italy into a disastrous war; another, a labor policy that made the workers seize the first opportunity to hasten his fall. In Spain, Perón saw not only a monument to the frightfulness of civil war but also a warning not to let fundamental antagonism develop between the nation's armed forces and organized labor, for this had been a major cause of the Spanish holocaust. Moreover, Spain's history in the 1920s suggested a solution attractive to a military man such as Perón. This was the partially successful effort of dictator Primo de Rivera to enlist labor support for his military regime. A similar effort in Argentina would have a better chance of success, if only because the great bulk of the Argentine labor force was as yet unorganized and could therefore be more easily manipulated than the comparatively old and strong Spanish unions.

In point of personality Perón was well fitted for his self-appointed task of creating a regime based on an alliance between the armed forces and a national labor force. In July 1945, when he was only four months short of fifty years of age, an unfriendly correspondent described him as looking "much younger" than that, with a ruddy complexion set off by black hair, "strong, vigorous . . . very smart and handsome in his uniform . . . endowed with great personal charm," and as speaking "well and convincingly, both in private conversation and in public." Ever the opportunist, Perón preferred to be all things to all men, but on occasion he could speak with the air of decision and authority acquired by a lifetime of command. Although his height was only medium and his arms embarrassingly short, these handicaps did not prevent him from becoming an expert swordsman and a worthy representative of the *macho* (he-man) type so highly esteemed in Argentina, by military and civilians alike. Though only a colonel (promoted in 1941), he soon rose to leadership in a G.O.U. that included several generals, and from the start he headed the colonels' clique that supplanted the G.O.U. early in 1944. His personality was an invaluable asset to him in his two main steps to political power, which were first to mobilize a manipulable labor force and then to procure the armed forces' acceptance of labor as an ally in a regime that would replace the dictatorship.

In both stages, and still more after they had been completed and the new regime set up in 1946, Perón owed his success in large part to the passionate devotion of that extraordinary woman, Eva Duarte, whom he married just after she helped to organize his rescue in the crisis of October 1945. Then twenty-five years old, she was just half his age. Her greatest public service to him was rendered in connection with the descamisados. She popularized his program among them and fixed in their minds the image of Perón as their unique benefactor and champion. This she accomplished first by her fiery speeches to the masses and later through personal contacts with them as head of the fabulously rich Eva Perón Foundation, in which role she became the leading lady bountiful of Argentina. Her own humble origins and her experience on stage, radio, and screen fitted her admirably for the role by instilling in her a deep hatred for the supercilious oligarchy, coupled with genuine sympathy for the "suffering masses," and by giving her the ability to harangue the descamisados movingly in their own language.

When Perón met Eva, she was only a kind of combination party girl, specializing in the military, and second-rate actress. Almost at once, however, she developed top-notch talent as a demagogue and a singleminded devotion to Perón that never flagged to the day of her death from cancer in 1952. In her innumerable speeches she did not hesitate to compare him with the national hero, the Liberator San Martín, to the latter's disadvantage. According to her, Perón was a second and greater San Martín, the San Martín of the people. She made her point: on May 7, 1952, a servile Congress actually conferred upon Perón the title "Liberator of the Republic." At the same time it declared Eva "Spiritual Chief of the Nation." She had in fact become the spiritual chief of the descamisados, and she used her headship to transmute the descamisados' political support of Perón into a cult, so that they would idolize him as she herself did. He had Eva to thank for the fact that, years after he deserted them and fled, he still retained the descamisados' devotion.

But this was not all. By taking descamisado demagoguery as her special province, Eva made possible a division of labor between herself and Perón that had two advantages for him. The first was that it enabled him to concentrate his own efforts on the other major sector of his program and pillar of his power, the military, and, in doing so, to maintain his role as an officer and a gentleman. He could speak as commonly, coarsely, and violently as she, and on occasion did so; but from the time she joined him until after her death, he usually worked one side of the street and she the other. The second advantage was that Eva's role in the regime helped to maintain its unstable equilibrium as between the descamisados and the military. It is also possible, though proof is lacking, that Eva exerted an even wider influence in helping Perón steer his regime on its difficult course. At any rate, soon after her death both he and his regime started on the downward path that led them to disaster within the next three years.

Mobilizing the Masses

Colonel Perón's marriage to a woman of Eva's antecedents was a challenge not only to the respectability of the old ruling classes but particularly to military decorum. The challenge must have been deliberate since it put into practice so flagrantly his program of remaking Argentine society by putting down the mighty and exalting the meek. Its central feature, the mobilization of the working class as a major power group under Perón's leadership, began to emerge in October 1943, when he added the headship of the Department of Labor and Social Security to the position he already held as chief of the Ministry of War's secretariat. Possession of these two posts greatly facilitated his plans for forging an alliance between the military and labor.

Perón worked with exemplary despatch. His methodology was as simple as it was effective. Backed by the force of the military dictatorship, he put a small army of labor organizers to work, some improvised, others drawn from the existing labor leadership. All were cajoled or coerced; those who refused to do his bidding were deprived of employment and blacklisted, and those who actively opposed were imprisoned and sometimes tortured. But he made more use of the carrot than the club. Dignity, freedom, and higher wages were his chief lures. These were seductive, for in the old Argentina workers had had no dignity and, since 1930, even the few who were organized had had little freedom in their own organizations and still less in collective bargaining to better their lot.

Under Perón's system, on the other hand, the unions debated

their problems freely, were permitted to strike and had government support when they did, and elected their own officials. To be sure, they must get Perón's advance approval of their strikes, and they must elect officials loyal to him; but who could object to that, when he was their great benefactor? And he lost no time in establishing himself in the benefactor's role: in December 1943 he issued a decree requiring all employers to pay their workers a bonus of one month's salary. No matter that it was already an established custom, widely practiced, to pay such bonuses; Perón was the one who made the payment obligatory and universal, and this was his Christmas present (*aguinaldo*) to the workers. More was to follow; indeed, he continued to shower wage increases, fringe benefits, and dignity on the workers until, pleading hard times, he called a halt in 1953, shortly after Eva's death.

On May 1, 1944, Perón held the first of the great May Day labor rallies in the Plaza de Mayo that were to become a fixture of his regime. His speech to the tens of thousands of cheering workers that packed the plaza was a paean of triumph. Contrasting their present happy state with the exploitation they had suffered up to 1943, he boasted that in the few months since he took office more had been done for them than ever before. But this was only the first stage, he said, and the fight for social justice would go on, at whatever cost, until victory had been won. Some two months later, in another address to the workers in this same square, he freely admitted that the benefits of his relationship to labor were reciprocal. He had just been elevated to the vice presidency, and he gave full credit for his promotion to the backing he had received from the workers. At the same time, he interpreted his promotion as proof that his campaign for social reform had President Farrell's full support, and this in turn as the best assurance that the workers would continue to add to their social gains.

Perón did not, however, at this time carry his championship of labor and government controls to the point of attacking capitalism and free enterprise. Nor was there as yet any suggestion of the anticlericalism that began to manifest itself in his regime after 1950. On May 30, 1944, for example, he said, "the representatives of capital and labor ought to adjust their relations to the most Christian rules of living together in mutual respect," and on October 15, 1944:

We do not support either the worker against sound capitalism, or monopolies against the working class; rather, we favor solutions equally beneficial to the workers and to commerce and industry, because our only interest is in the welfare of our fatherland [*patria*].

Why, then, his championship of the masses at this juncture? Because, he said on June 10, 1944, "The agitation of the masses is a result of social injustice. The remedy lies in giving them justice."

Nationalism was one of his major themes from the start, and he linked it to social reform. On December 2, 1943, in his first speech after the elevation of his labor post to cabinet rank, he said:

In defending those who suffer and labor to give substance and form to the nation's greatness, I am defending the *patria* in accordance with an oath I took in which I pledged my life. And life is little to offer on the altar of the *patria*.

At this time his definition of the *patria* stressed Church and Army and their historic union. As he put it on June 28, 1944:

The Argentine Republic is a product of Hispanic colonization and conquest, which brought to our land, in brotherly union and with a single will, the cross and the sword. And in the present situation there appears to be taking place again that extraordinary conjunction of spiritual forces and power represented by . . . the gospel and the sword.

If these comparatively mild pronouncements were sincere, why did Perón apply the term "revolution" to what he and his associates were about? And why were they so bitterly opposed both at home and abroad? The answer is partly that, as Perón himself often said publicly, actions speak louder than words, and partly that on occasion he used words of a very different tenor.

An especially notable occasion of this kind was Perón's sensational speech on June 10, 1944, in which he asserted that it made little difference to Argentina whether the Axis or the Allies won the war, and that Argentina's legitimate national aspirations could be realized only by her own efforts and through a combination of diplomacy, military power, and "total" organization of the nation. His words were a challenge to many, both at home and abroad. Most challenging of all was his use of the word "total," which was taken to connote totalitarian designs at home and pro-Axis sympathies abroad. Its effect was heightened by the critical state of the war at that time. Only four days earlier the Allies had made a landing in Normandy; only two days before that, Perón's military mentor, General Carlos von der Becke, had delivered a lecture to the Argentine officers in which he declared that no such operation could succeed; and it was too early to be sure whether the General was right or wrong. In this tense situation, Perón's speech sounded like a vote of confidence in Hitler's armed forces and the totalitarian system. As such, it cancelled out most of what he had said, and would go on saying, in a different vein.

Yet Perón's more moderate pronouncements served him well in Argentina until he was safely entrenched in the presidency, in 1946, and could proceed more openly. Their chief merit lay in the fact that he made them plausible enough to win him the support of some leaders in labor and politics who would never have taken his side if they had foreseen how he was going to betray them once he had been elected. Until then, he needed all the support he could get, for his margin of victory was razor-thin in the crisis of October 1945 and none too wide in the presidential election four months later. Against him he had nearly all the newspapers, business and professional organizations, university students and faculty, and all the old political parties, which were banned in 1943, but continued *sub rosa* until they were permitted to come out into the open again late in 1945.

From Prison to Presidency

Only the highlights of the story of Perón's success in the face of these odds can be given here. The story falls into two interrelated parts, foreign and domestic. The foreign part need not detain us. It revolves mainly about Argentina's relations with the United States and is notable mainly for two reasons: first, because the United States' effort to unhorse the pro-Axis rulers in Buenos Aires, though based mainly on inter-American agreements, failed through its inability to obtain the full cooperation of a non-American power, Great Britain; and second, because this effort, which continued through Argentina's election of 1946, took on the aspect of a duel between Perón and U.S. Assistant Secretary of State Spruille Braden, thus enabling Perón to attract nationalist votes as the champion of Argentine independence against Yankee intervention.

On the home front Perón's first major test began in June 1945 and culminated in October, when he was first imprisoned and then, after eight days, brought back in triumph. This was soon followed by his second major test, a presidential campaign, from which he likewise emerged victorious—to the surprise of most of his foes.

The end of the war in Europe in May 1945 raised a clamor in Argentina for the restoration of constitutional government. Emboldened by the destruction of the Nazi and fascist regimes, enemies of their Argentine counterpart launched a campaign of manifestoes, rumors, and demonstrations against it. Their heaviest fire was concentrated on Perón as an instigator of class conflict and economic heresies. He jumped at the chance to fight it out on this line and replied with the warning that he now had on his side a labor "army" of four million organized workingmen.

In fact, however, Perón's position within the regime itself was not secure, for he was still only second in command, under President Farrell, and many of his military associates had as much aversion as any civilian oligarch for Perón's program of social revolution. On October 9 he was brought to the brink of disaster when a group of them led by General Eduardo Avalos, commanding officer of the big Campo de Mayo garrison on the outskirts of Buenos Aires, "detained" him and sent him to the traditional place of detention for political prisoners, the island of Martin García in the Plata estuary.

The friends of freedom now had a chance to remake the regime, but they bungled the opportunity badly. As has so often happened in similar situations in Latin American countries, they promptly fell to quarrelling among themselves over the succession. Perón's supporters, on the other hand, quickly prepared a counterstroke. With the help of the Buenos Aires police, this was delivered on October 17 in the form of a carefully organized "spontaneous" demonstration by a horde of workers shouting "Bring back Perón" and threatening to tear Buenos Aires apart if they were denied. Eva Duarte (not yet Eva Perón) was one of the organizers; another was Cipriano Reyes, head of the slaughter-house workers, whose presence in the demonstration helped the threats of a general blood-letting carry conviction. It was this occasion that gave currency to the term *descamisado;* first applied to the "shirtless" demonstrators by Perón's enemies as an opprobrious epithet, the term was adopted by the Peronists as a badge of honor.

Faced with the alternative of either yielding or firing on the demonstrators and quite possibly starting a civil war, Perón's military foes gave in and brought him back in triumph the same day. But the upshot was not a complete surrender on their part but a compromise which foreshadowed the sharing of power between the military and labor in the Perón regime. On the one hand, Perón resigned all his posts in the government and his commission as colonel (after his election he regained it as a general). On the other hand, he now came out openly as a candidate for the presidency with an unqualified commitment to his controversial promises of sweeping social reforms.

On the evening of this momentous October 17, speaking from a balcony of the executive mansion, the Casa Rosada, Perón told the cheering descamisados massed in the Plaza de Mayo, "I have resigned from the army in order to help revive the almost forgotten civilian tradition of Argentina and join with the sweating, suffering mass of laborers who are building the greatness of this nation." At the end of his fifteen-minute speech, he urged the descamisados to leave quietly and get back to work, as he himself planned to do after a brief and well-earned rest. Four days later he made Eva Duarte his wife in a secret civil ceremony; six weeks later the union was publicly sealed in a church wedding.

The ensuing presidential campaign again illustrated the internal divisions and other weaknesses of the forces opposed to Perón. Most of the older parties formed a coalition called the Democratic Union, but bickered too long over the choice of a candidate and then came up with a colorless figure, a sixty-year-old lawyer and former cabinet minister under Alvear, José Tamborini. Their platform promised reform, but not enough of it; and in any case the masses had little or no confidence in these old-line parties—that was one reason for Perón's popularity. To make matters still worse, the Radicals, the largest of the coalition parties, were split as usual. One of their three factions sulked in its tents and another supported Perón. He also had the support of two labor parties and was the beneficiary of a pastoral letter in which the Catholic hierarchy forbade the faithful to vote for any candidate of a party favoring divorce and secular education, as did the Democratic Union.

During the campaign the Democratic Union suffered harassment such as violence by thugs at political rallies and interference with deliveries of political mail by postal employees sympathetic to Perón. In the main, however, it campaigned freely, by radio and otherwise; it had the support of most of the newspapers; and its leaders were so confident of victory that at least one of them predicted a Peronist coup to forestall the election.

Duly held on February 24, 1946, the election was, according to the best evidence, free and honest. It gave Perón a majority small enough to sustain the impression of its freedom and honesty but large enough to make his victory clearcut. Of the 2,734,386 votes cast, he received 1,527,231, or 56 per cent. In the Electoral College, similar to that in the United States, he received 304 votes to Tamborini's 72, carrying all but four of the provinces, of which the only populous one was Córdoba. His party also won two thirds of the seats in the Chamber of Deputies and an even larger proportion in the Senate. It is generally agreed that this surprising victory was won largely with descamisado votes, but little note has been taken of the fact that, as nearly as can be determined, these came not only from voters who switched from the older parties but also from men who had not previously voted. At any rate, whereas only 41 per cent of the adult male population had voted in 1928, and 48 per cent in 1937, the figure rose to 56 per cent in 1946.

With a six-year term lying ahead of him, Perón now had enough of the instruments of power in his hands to proceed with the "total" organization of the nation called for in his sensational speech of June 10, 1944. In the last stage, the election of 1946, he achieved this position through a constitutional, democratic process, and he was to continue to act with a nice regard for the forms of law. But the use he was to make of his growing power only showed how the letter can kill the spirit.

SEVEN

PERONIST HIGH TIDE

1946-1949

On June 4, 1946, the third anniversary of the armed forces' seizure of power under G.O.U. leadership, Juan Perón was inaugurated as president with suitable éclat but otherwise uneventfully. In the next three years his regime reached its peak in every respect. These sunshine years were marked by economic prosperity in all sectors except agriculture, by the extension and tightening of the regime's hold on the country, and by a recovery of the rather considerable role that Argentina had played in international affairs for some time before 1939 but had lost in the following few years.

Before the period was over, Perón and his associates had produced a distinctive amalgam of doctrine and policy under the labels Justicialism and Third Position. Its stated objectives were social justice, economic independence, and complete national sovereignty. These were to be achieved by combining the best features of socialism with those of the capitalist–free enterprise system, and by following a foreign policy of noncommitment, which Perón insisted was not a rigid, sterile neutralism. And to operate his system and execute his program, he built up what was in effect a highly centralized government under a single party, with himself standing at the summit in the combined role of peerless leader, chief of state, and object of a pseudo-religious cult.

The important differences between this neo-fascist system and the European originals have already been pointed out. As will be shown below, the differences consisted mainly of modifications in terms of

Argentine environment and traditions. For a time these gave it a strong appeal in Argentina. But its significance far transcends the limits of that country, for it anticipated the national liberation type of movement that has subsequently found favor in other Latin American countries and elsewhere in the world. Even in the years of its pristine power, however, Perón's regime began to reveal the weaknesses that were ultimately to wreck it, and at the same time revealed some fragments of strength that were to survive that fortunate disaster.

Another Gilded Age

Perón came in on a high wave of prosperity. In a society dominated by such a government as his, the inevitable result was the creation of a gilded age atmosphere of extravagant display, tasteless pretension, and corruption on a grand scale reminiscent of the gaudy 1880s. One aspect of it was symbolized by Perón and Eva themselves in their wardrobes. Returning from a trip to Europe in 1947, this creole Cinderella brought back trunkloads of ermine capes, mink coats, gowns designed by the *haute couture* of Paris, and other feminine apparel. Her annual clothing bill is said to have reached $40,000. Perón, when he fled the country incontinently in 1955, left behind 200 suits, 83 pairs of shoes, 10 pairs of riding boots, 90 hats and military caps, and hundreds of shirts and neckties. By this time there remained very few other Argentines, even among Perón's well-rewarded favorites, who could maintain the earlier pace of conspicuous consumption, for after 1949 prosperity vanished, never to return. With its going, the gilded age lost its gilt, and only its vices remained.

Because of its sources, this prosperity could not have been sustained at the same high level indefinitely, though moderately good management would have made the following slump much less severe. Its chief source was the booming postwar market in Europe for Argentine foodstuffs; this was bound to contract as reconstruction brought Europe's own production of foodstuffs back to normal. The other important source was Argentina's large wartime accumulation of gold and foreign exchange balances (the latter largely in sterling); these amounted in 1946 to some $1,600 million and accounted for more than one third of the total reserves of this kind held by all the Latin

American countries combined. For any Latin American country, this was a fabulous treasure, but the foreign exchange balances were a wasting asset. They had been built up because during the war foreign purchasers of Argentine products had been unable to make payment in the goods desired by Argentina. Now that the war was over, the balances had to be unfrozen and spent quickly, for their purchasing power declined as prices rose. By putting them to productive uses, a higher level of economic activity could have been maintained, but that was not done.

That Perón missed this golden opportunity was not for lack of ambitious designs. These were first set forth in his Five-Year plan of 1947. The plan had three major objectives. One was to nationalize the foreign-owned railways, river steamship lines, and public utilities by purchase, not by confiscation or expropriation. The object was to promote Argentina's economic independence without alienating the country's trading partners. Economic independence was sought both as a matter of national pride and for practical purposes, such as shifting control to Argentine hands and keeping the profits at home. The second objective was to accelerate the industrialization of Argentina. Here again economic independence was a stated goal, but so also were social improvements, through the increase of per capita wealth, and national defense, particularly through the development of heavy industry, with the military playing a leading role. In the third place, Argentina's wealth was to be used to build up the nation's international power and prestige. This had been one of the G.O.U.'s major objectives when it seized power in 1943, and it was still one of Perón's. Thus, nationalism, whether political or economic, was the dominant note in all the three principal aspects of his policy.

When his sunshine years ran out in 1949, Perón had achieved his first objective and had met with some success in the other two, but at a ruinous cost. He had acquired the foreign-owned railways, telephones, gas companies, Buenos Aires streetcar system, and various port installations, and had repatriated the foreign debt. In the process, however, he had exhausted the reserves and drawn heavily on IAPI (see below), to the great injury of the key sector of the national economy, agriculture and stockraising; and the chief acquisition, the foreign-owned railways, had turned out to be a white elephant. As for industrialization, progress was made in the already

well developed field of consumer goods, as shown by a 31 per cent
increase from 1946 to 1949 in the value of manufactures; but in
heavy industry the basic project, the building of a big modern steel
mill, remained a pipe dream to the very end in 1955. The gross
national product (total of all goods and services), which was already rising rapidly when Perón took office, continued its sharp
ascent through the next two years, reaching its peak for the whole
Perón period in 1948. The next year showed a slight drop,* which
turned out to be the beginning of a disastrous four-year decline, but
this was not foreseen at the time and the sense of well-being, achievement, and confidence continued to prevail through 1949.

In international affairs, Argentina now regained its prominence of
the 1930s. At the time of the Soviet blockade of Berlin in 1948, for
example, Argentine Foreign Minister Juan Atilio Bramuglia was
chairman of the United Nations Security Council and spokesman
for its six "neutral" members who sought to work out a compromise
solution. Earlier that year Argentina's representative at the United
Nations Conference on Trade and Employment, at Havana, made
the headlines by casting his government in the role of champion of
Latin America against Yankee imperialism. He announced that his
government was prepared to provide five billion dollars for the economic development of the rest of Latin America, whereas the United
States was not only refusing Latin America an equivalent of its
Marshall Plan aid to Europe, but was even trying to cripple the
Latin Americans' infant industries by involving them in a general
reduction of protective tariffs. One of Perón's most gratifying successes came when in 1947 the Hemisphere defense conference, post-
poned in 1945 at Washington's behest as a slap at Perón, was after
all held (at Rio de Janeiro), with his government playing a leading
role. By this time, the Cold War was in full swing and the United
States was willing to let bygones be bygones with Perón; but in accordance with his Third Position, he maintained an aloof attitude
for several years to come, departing from it only to denounce Yankee
imperialism. That he could afford to do so was a source of pride to
many Argentines besides Perón.

* Argentina's gross national product in billions of pesos at 1950 prices was
41.5 in 1945, 47.6 in 1946, 55.8 in 1947, 62.3 in 1948, and 60.9 in 1949. The
1950 peso was worth about 7 cents in U.S. money.

These gains in prestige, however, were counterbalanced by practical failures much nearer home. Democratic Uruguay remained a
thorn in his side and a place of refuge, plotting, and propaganda for
his Argentine enemies. He was never able to establish his influence
over Bolivia and Paraguay on a firm basis. Big Brazil was cool toward
him, and Chile cautiously tepid. Thus he was balked in his designs
for hegemony in southern South America; and he had no luck at all
with his projected formation of a bloc of all the Latin American
nations.

It is ironical that Perón made economics the basis of his interpretation of history and human nature, and gave it top priority in his
policy, for he showed himself quite incompetent in the economic
field. This was one of the two chief weaknesses of his administration
even in its palmy days; the other was corruption, and both continued
to haunt his regime to the end. Two of his most important early
measures illustrate both defects. One was the establishment in 1946
of the Argentine Institute for the Promotion of Trade, called IAPI
from the initials of its name in Spanish. Before long, critics were
saying with reason that it would more properly have been called
"Institute for the Suppression of Agriculture." A government agency,
it had a monopoly of the purchase, at its own price, of meat and all
major crops, of their sale abroad, and of the purchase, with the
proceeds, of machinery and other goods not only for itself but also
for all other Argentine agencies. The conception was bad, the execution worse, and the results disastrous. Domestic farm prices were
forced down to a level that destroyed incentive, and while sales
abroad during the boom period yielded handsome profits, these were
in large part wasted or misappropriated. The most disastrous result
was the crippling of agriculture. One indication was the reduction
of the area under cultivation from an average of 21.5 million hectares in 1934-44 to a little less than 19 million hectares in 1949,
although population was increasing rapidly. In 1952 Argentina,
formerly one of the world's largest exporters of wheat, became an
importer. The adverse effect of Perón's measures on the international
position of Argentina was not fully revealed until after 1949, but it
was already beginning to show, for the country's capacity to import
was now slightly lower than it had been a decade earlier.

The other example is the purchase in 1948 of the foreign-owned railways. Most of these, comprising 65 per cent of the total Argentine network, were British, and the rest were French or Argentine. All the lines were badly run down, most of them nearly if not quite bankrupt, and the owners eager to sell. As a result, the price paid for them, some $600 million (£120 million for the British, 5,500 million francs for the French), seemed generous and even munificent, and gave rise to charges of bribery and corruption that have never been cleared up. They are not necessarily true, for Perón may have paid the price simply because he was eager to close the deal and present the country with a dramatic achievement in his campaign for Argentina's economic independence. But even if the price was right and the negotiation immaculate, the money could have been put to better and more productive use; for example, to continue the highway construction program begun in the 1930s, or to give more reality to Perón's much-heralded industrialization program, or to help agriculture in one way or another.

Even assuming that the foreign railway purchase was a political necessity for a government based so largely on the appeal to nationalism, it would seem that Perón was unwise to pay the full amount at once, as he did, thereby virtually exhausting Argentina's wartime accumulation of foreign exchange. A better alternative would have been to insist on an installment purchase plan, as he was in a position to do, for this would have left a large part of the accumulated foreign credits at his disposal for the rehabilitation of railway tracks and equipment. Such rehabilitation had been long neglected and was now a crying need. Even in 1940, more than one third of the railway engines were at least 38 years old, and an equal number between 14 and 37 years old, and virtually no new ones had been acquired since 1940. The other equipment and tracks were in a like state of decrepitude.

Instead, Perón bought this gigantic one-horse shay at an inflated price for cash on the barrel-head and then not only let it continue to run down but accelerated its ruin by packing its staff with deserving Peronists. As a result, the Argentine railways soon became a prime example of bureaucratic politics, featherbedding, and incompetence. After his fall, they constituted one of Argentina's gravest problems; before his fall, even the regime, while not admitting its error, had stopped boasting about their acquisition. This was celebrated with great fanfare on every March 1 for several years, but by 1955 the celebrations had become such an obviously hollow mockery that they were abandoned.

Similar stories could be told of other developments of the Perón regime's early years, such as its purchase (and the sequel) of the United River Plate Telephone Company (a subsidiary of the International Telephone and Telegraph Company), and about the seemingly strange neglect of that prime symbol of Argentine nationalism, Y.P.F. But further details would only confirm conclusions already indicated: that in the economic field Perón was a bungler whose nationalism was more extreme in words than deeds and whose tyranny was tempered by corruption.

Perón the Peerless Leader

Far more adept in politics than economics, and brilliantly seconded by Eva, Perón in his first term was his country's most popular leader since Irigoyen; only a minority, about one third of the people, held out against him. More than this, he was exceptionally skillful as well as ruthless in capitalizing on his popularity and the prosperity of his early years in power. They were used to tighten his control of both the country at large and his own following, and yet at the same time to preserve the fiction that he was acting constitutionally and democratically in the best Argentine tradition. As part of the process he made simply-worded pronouncements of Peronist "doctrine" packaged for maximum popular appeal.

When Perón's presidential term began, he still had a long way to go in order to establish complete control over the country. He lost no time in starting on that journey. In accordance with a broad hint in his first inaugural address, the uncooperative Supreme Court was purged, not by violence or dictatorial decree but by the constitutional process of impeachment carried out by his henchmen in Congress. In April 1947, all the judges were thus removed except one who had played ball with the regime, and the vacancies were then filled with Peronists. The inferior courts were later purged under one of the articles of the amended Constitution of 1949. The universities too were "renovated," as Peronists put it. Their purging since 1943 had been sporadic and temporary, but it now became systematic and definitive. In May 1946 the government "intervened" all of the country's six universities, that is, it placed government-appointed interventors in control of them. This was followed in the closing months of the year by a wholesale purge of their faculties: 1,250 faculty members, or 70 per cent of the total, were dismissed, retired, or otherwise eliminated. The next year a new University Law deprived the universities of autonomy for the avowed purpose of making it impossible for them ever again to "oppose the will of the Argentine people," i.e., the Peronists. Similar treatment was meted out to the students.

Other steps toward establishing total control involved the opposition parties, the radio network, the press, and organized labor. Although the pretense of political freedom was kept up, critics of the regime were increasingly harassed in a number of ways, including prosecutions for *desacato* (disrespect) and denial of the use of the radio stations, all of which were now brought under government control. Freedom of the press was destroyed, not, as a rule, by frontal assault but by punitive measures in individual cases, such as the cutting off of newsprint supplies (a government monopoly), the imposition of fines for alleged violations of sanitary and building codes, and, for those who still remained recalcitrant, condemnation proceedings in court.

As for organized labor, it had not been brought completely to heel at the time of Perón's inauguration. Some of its leaders had supported him in his rise to power on the naive assumption that they and the unions would retain their freedom after his election. When they found that, on the contrary, they were to be integrated into the Peronist movement and dominated by Perón, they resisted. He soon disposed of them. The case of Cipriano Reyes is typical. He had aided Perón greatly both on the crucial October 17 and in the ensuing presidential election, but when he opposed the absorption of his labor party by the Peronist movement, Perón first broke him both as a political and a labor leader, and then, when he continued to carp, threw him into jail, where he remained until Perón's overthrow. But in general more use was made of persuasion than of force. The mass of workers enjoyed the substantial benefit of an increase of 34 per cent in real wages between 1945 and 1949, and labor leaders were rewarded with good posts in appropriate organizations such as the

C.G.T., the nationalized railways, and the Peronist party, as well as in departments of the government itself.

Perón's hold over his followers was strengthened both by rewards for their support and also by two institutional changes. In the former category, he was generous during his regime's flush years to the rank and file of its two main pillars, the armed forces and labor, and most generous to their leaders. While all the military benefited, and even the common soldiers were given higher pay and better barracks, a special effort was made to Peronize the sergeants, for Perón, quite rightly as it proved, did not wholly trust the commissioned officers. Among other concessions, the sergeants were provided with a new kind of uniform which was more like an officer's than an enlisted man's; seemingly inconsequential, this was a shrewd appeal to the well-developed Argentine sense of dignity. The officers, too, received pay increases, and in addition were appointed to profitable posts in the increasingly numerous enterprises that were either state-owned or of a mixed government-private character. Another reward for specially favored officers was import licenses—increasingly valuable as import controls tightened after the brief boom period.

Eva Perón aided greatly in making masses of people feel indebted to the regime for both practical benefits and dignity. Equal rights for women was her first major mission. For years a feminist movement had been going on in Argentina, but it had never made much progress and in the first phase of the revolution of 1943, when conservative Catholic influence was strong, it had suffered a setback. Eva took it up and carried it to a quick victory. The central measure, votes for women, was enacted in 1947, and women voted in the next national election, in 1951.

Even more important for the regime—and characteristic of Eva— was her social welfare work through an ostensibly private organization, the María Eva Duarte de Perón Foundation. Established in 1948 on a small scale with her own funds and voluntary contributions from others, the Foundation mushroomed rapidly as pressure added "voluntary" contributions from business firms and other organizations. These were in effect protection money, and one firm that had the temerity to refuse to pay up was fined heavily on trumped-up charges and forced into bankruptcy. The C.G.T. contributed $6 million per year, which came from what amounted to a wage tax on its members. Even the government contributed from its lottery proceeds, but it still kept up the pretense that the Foundation was private, and accordingly exercised no control or supervision over it.

Yet a large part of the Foundation's funds were spent on useful purposes, such as the building of hospitals, playgrounds, and many schools. Also, Eva, who worked hard at her job, spent many hours every day in individual interviews with the poor, whom she aided with advice and in more practical ways. She and her Foundation thus supplanted the country's leading charitable organization, the century-old Society of Philanthropy, formerly maintained by the ladies of the oligarchy. But Eva rejected the word charitable: in the new Argentina, she declared, the poor do not receive charity but only what is rightly theirs by the standards of social justice. This, more than anything else, explains why *Eva dignifica* ("Eva dignifies") was the inscription under the picture of her on posters plastered all over the country. The same posters bore a portrait of Perón, and the inscription underneath his was *Perón cumple,* meaning "Perón does what he promises" or "Peron delivers the goods."

One of the two institutional changes referred to above was the founding of the Peronist party. This did not take place until just after the election of 1946. Previously, Perón had rejected the idea of creating such a party, for at first he joined with the rest of the G.O.U. in condemning the whole party system. Even after he developed a political following of his own he continued for a time to insist that it was a national movement above party strife, as Irigoyen had done in the case of the Radical Party. But Perón's decision to maintain a pretense of constitutional democracy, complete with elections and opposition parties, forced him to reverse his original position and found a party of his own, though he never gave up the claim that his national movement was more than a party.

At first the new party was relatively large and loosely organized and was called the Single Party of the Revolution, but after three years' experience it was completely reorganized for greater centralization and tighter discipline by a party convention of already well-disciplined delegates who completed their task in a single day (July 25, 1949). Illustrating the increasingly personalist character of the regime, the name was changed to Peronist Party (*partido peronista*). As in Communist parties, membership was made a privilege restricted to a small minority, and the number of members was kept secret; a credible estimate placed it between 250,000 and 300,000. All these were men; a separate Peronist party was soon established for the newly enfranchised women. The penalty for a breach of party discipline was expulsion, which had almost the effect of excommunication in past ages. At the controls of this machine stood Perón himself, as president of the men's party, and Eva, of the women's.

Earlier the same year Perón made the other important institutional change, a "reform" of the Constitution of 1853. The change was made by a convention elected for the purpose, as prescribed by the existing constitution, and this convention, unlike the party convention that was soon to meet, made a show of serious deliberation, remaining in session from January 24 to March 11, 1949. That it behaved like a rubber-stamp body is not surprising, since its chairman, Domingo Mercante, had been one of Perón's chief lieutenants from the start and the Peronist members outnumbered the opposition (all Radicals) 109 to 48. Except in overruling Perón's *pro forma* objection to an amendment making him eligible for re-election, the convention produced a document that might just as well have been written by Perón himself.

Of greatest immediate importance among the amendments was the one just mentioned. Another abolished the Electoral College and provided for direct election of the president and vice president by popular vote. Still others wrote Perón's social program into the constitution, expanded government control over the economy at the expense of private enterprise, declared all minerals and almost all natural sources of power the property of the nation, and provided for government ownership of all "public services" (without defining the term).

Some of these innovations seemed to augur the adoption of a still more revolutionary course by the regime. Yet in other respects the "reformed" constitution was strikingly conservative and was in fact simply a re-enactment of the existing constitution. Like the latter, it described the government of Argentina as federal, republican, and representative; distributed powers between the central government and the provinces; provided for a threefold separation of powers (executive, legislative, and judicial) and vested these in a president, a bicameral Congress, and a federal judiciary. Last but not least, it continued the old church-state relationship, which required the government to support the Roman Catholic Church.

Justicialism and the Third Position

With an amended constitution that broadened his powers and made him eligible for re-election, and a renovated party to get him re-elected, Perón was in a stronger political position than ever before at the close of 1949. His position was probably also strengthened by his two recent formulations of his regime's doctrine. One was the Declaration of Economic Independence adopted in Tucumán by representatives of the people and government on July 9, 1947, at a celebration of the one hundred and thirty-first anniversary of Argentina's declaration of political independence at the same place. Asserting their "will to be economically free," as the earlier declaration had proclaimed Argentina's political sovereignty, the signers specified what they meant by this new freedom: "economic emancipation from the foreign capitalist powers that have exercised control" over Argentina and from "those in the country who have been linked with them." In other words, this was a declaration of war on what at other times Peronist leaders labelled the unholy alliance between foreign economic imperialism and Argentina's own *vendepatria* oligarchy. It therefore had great significance for domestic as well as foreign policy and appealed not only to Argentine nationalists but also to descamisado resentment against the nation's privileged classes.

The second formulation, much more comprehensive than the first, was the doctrine of Justicialism (*justicialismo*) and the Third Position which Perón himself unveiled for the first time in April 1949 at an international philosophical meeting in Mendoza. Appearing there in the role of philosopher, Perón read a paper in which, after a learned discussion of nineteenth-century German thought, he addressed himself to the problem of collectivism versus individualism. His conclusion was the not very novel one that extremes in either direction were wrong and that a middle ground was needed. But he showed a talent worthy of Madison Avenue in inventing catchy labels: Third Position for the middle ground, and Justicialism for the body of doctrine appropriate to it.

Although Perón's first statement of these ideas was rather sketchy, the labels caught on at once. This was not because of any great public interest in the philosophical problems involved but because the state of affairs in Argentina and the world at large made many Argentines highly receptive to the ideas suggested by the labels. To them, "Third Position" meant a compromise between totalitarianism and unfettered free enterprise, and abstention from any foreign commitment that would deprive Argentina of freedom of action in the Cold War; and "Justicialism" connoted primarily social justice at home, though international justice too was understood.

Soon realizing that they had a political bonanza, Peronist leaders quickly expanded these implications into a full-blown "national doctrine" and gave it headline billing for the rest of the regime's life. They often used the labels interchangeably, but "Justicialism" had the greater vogue, partly because it was verbally more flexible (Third Position, for example, could not readily be turned into an adjective or the name of a group) and partly because usage tended to confine "Third Position" to foreign and economic policy. Perón's name was, of course, constantly coupled with both. "Peronist Justicialism," for example, was the term used to identify the list of the new national doctrine's "twenty truths" when he featured it in a major speech on October 17, 1950.

Many commentators on the Perón period have treated Justicialism roughly. One of them, Alejandro Magnet, writes that the regime was never able to rise above the "doctrinal primitivism" of its early days, that in its later years it "covered its ideological nakedness with increasingly pretentious and rhetorical vestments," and that under this covering there was never anything substantial except the personality of Perón. This view is correct as far as it goes, but it does not go nearly far enough. When Perón and his henchmen fabricated Justicialism, they were engaging not in an intellectual exercise but in a struggle for power. For that purpose Justicialism served them well. Another commentator, George Blanksten, has pointed out that as "a doctrine of the balancing of forces" it was theoretically well suited to the needs of a regime constantly engaged in balancing the mutually antagonistic forces that composed it, such as the descamisados and the armed forces. As he further notes, Justicialism also served to disguise the regime's resemblance to the now discredited Nazi-fascist system, and its very lack of precision and finish made it an ideal framework for Perón's always opportunistic policies. It should be added that through Justicialism and the Declaration of Economic Independence Perón was able to make a host of Argentines believe that they were embarked with him in a great enterprise which was Argentine in conception and which had noble goals, chief among them social justice and national grandeur. That those who took this view were badly fooled is beside the point. The important thing is that they took it, and that in many of them— one third of the nation—the belief in Perón and Justicialism was so deeply implanted that it has survived his fall and flight nearly a decade, and is still strong.

If Perón himself had had faith in his doctrine and if he had remained steadfast in it against adversity, he might have held on to power indefinitely, as the amended constitution of 1949 permitted him to do. Instead, as the next chapter will show, while his cohorts were busy making Justicialism a secular religion to be instilled into all Argentines, the opportunistic Perón let heavy pressures at home and abroad lead him into one departure after another from his professed principles, until, in 1955, the most flagrant of all led straight to his overthrow.

EIGHT

PERÓN HESITATES AND IS LOST

1949-1955

In retrospect, it seems obvious that the Perón regime's almost unbroken succession of bad luck and increasingly bad management after 1950 headed it straight to the disaster that overtook it in September 1955. In 1950 a deep economic depression set in. In 1951 a military revolt, though suppressed, and a strike, though broken, raised doubts about the dependability of the regime's two main pillars, and a shamelessly rigged election proved even to the most gullible that its pretensions to democracy were a sham. In 1952 Perón lost his right arm in the death of Eva. The next year two policy changes weakened his popular support: a shift to sound economic policy, which involved a stoppage of handouts to the descamisados; and the beginning of a rapprochement with the United States. In 1954 he launched an attack on his former ally, the Roman Catholic Church, in terms that accentuated the totalitarian character of his regime. In 1955 he betrayed his regime's most basic principle, economic nationalism, through petroleum concessions to the Standard Oil Company of California. In September of that year he was ousted.

That Perón marched for five years straight to disaster may be fact, not fancy, but if so the fact is easier to see in hindsight than it was at the time. Thus, even Walter M. Beveraggi Allende, an Argentine exile who was one of the first observers to record the opinion that the Perón regime faced a grave crisis, wrote as late as

September 1954 that "we cannot predict what its consequences will be."

Why the crisis ended in Perón's fall can be explained in three ways. Though each of these can stand by itself and one or another will be given the greatest weight, depending on the weigher, they are not mutually exclusive and all three should be taken into account. According to one of them, the root cause of Perón's disaster was the deep economic depression of the early 1950s, which exacerbated antagonisms within the regime and pushed Perón into the errors that wrecked it. The second explanation pictures the regime as undone by the working out of its own inner logic and relegates economic developments to second place as mere circumstances of an inevitable process. Justicialism, it holds, was essentially a balancing system for the regime's own ill-assorted component groups; but as such Perón's character doomed it to failure, for whenever his position was threatened, he upset the balance by applying his divide-and-rule tactics to his own following as well as to the opposition. The third view is that Perón was undone by a failure of will. His lack of constancy, conviction, and courage and his shallow opportunism always made him indecisive in the great crises. The final crisis illustrates the point: In August 1955, he threatened to take bloody reprisals on the foes of the regime if they dared strike, but when they called his bluff by starting the blood-letting, he hesitated too long and was lost.

Economic Woes

However Perón's fall may be explained, there can be no question that the first unmistakable sign of serious trouble was the economic decline, which began in 1949 and by 1952 had become almost a collapse. Such phenomena are commonly measured by statistics, but this one can also be measured by rhetoric. On July 29, 1947, when the economy was booming, Perón delivered a speech in which he gave top priority to material well-being in his scale of values, saying:

> Why do we want economic independence? We want it in order to reconquer the nation's sources of wealth so that we may distribute it among the 16,000,000 inhabitants. Why do we want this increase in wealth? So as to elevate the "standard" [in English] of living and

to give the people an ever greater economic well-being and moral perfection. It is useless to talk to the people of spiritual or moral values when they are hungry. People have to be talked to after they have eaten, for the stomach, after the pocketbook, is the most sensitive of a man's vitals.

Five years later, at the depth of the depression, he turned this scale of values upside down. On May 1, 1952, in his annual message to Congress on the state of the union, he declared that excessive preoccupation with material welfare had frequently caused "great misfortune and the decadence of nations," and that the "supreme objective" of his government's campaign for social justice was to "dignify the workers" by bringing about "a just distribution of spiritual and moral benefits."

But cold statistics, too, are on hand to tell the story. The gross national product dropped from 62.3 billion pesos in 1948 to 49.3 in 1952. This meant a sharp decline in per capita wealth, since during these same years the population grew from about 15.4 million to 18 million. Even the favored manufacturing sector slumped and the value of farm products was cut in half. Worst of all, exports, which paid for vital imports, plummeted in 1952.

These economic woes were not entirely the government's fault, and it had some gains to its credit. Severe droughts from 1949 to 1951 cut grain production. The terms of trade were less favorable to Argentina after 1947, for the prices paid for imported manufactures rose whereas the prices received for Argentina's food exports declined, except for a brief revival in 1950-1951 because of the Korean war. The government's modest list of achievements included increases in some lines of industrial production, the building of oil and gas pipelines, and the discovery of coal and iron deposits, but was headed by the rapid growth of the Argentine State Merchant Fleet. In 1951, for the first time in history, more Argentine freight was shipped under the Argentine flag than under any foreign flag. Here was gratification for national pride, and some of the ships' names pointed to where credit was due: *Eva Perón, October 17,* and not only *Presidente Perón,* but also *Juan Perón.*

In most respects, however, the Argentine economy presented a dreary picture when the first Five-Year Plan was wound up in 1952. The country was suffering from serious shortages of power, raw materials, parts and replacements for worn-out machinery. The railroads were worse run down than ever, and, because of a dozen years of war and import restrictions, motor vehicles were too few and antiquated to supply the deficiency. Even favored Buenos Aires had an indigent, down-at-heels look at this time to one who had seen it in the booming days just before World War II, when the now discredited oligarchy was in control. And nothing had been done to fulfill two major promises: to build a big, modern steel mill, and to carry out an agrarian reform that would break up the big estates.

Girding up its loins, the regime came forth with a new and better Five-Year Plan for the period 1952-1957, and nature helped by smiling again. Yet when the facts came to light after the regime's fall, its record in its last three years was still a sorry one. Its proudest boast, an eleventh-hour resumption of industrial growth, was due to a fortunate combination of circumstances that could hardly be repeated. These included the backlog of demand built up during the years of deep depression and increases both in tariff protection and also, thanks to better crops, in consumer purchasing power. Moreover, even in rate of industrial growth Argentina in 1955 was being left far behind by other Latin American countries, especially Brazil, Venezuela, and Mexico, where the growth was not sporadic but had gone on from year to year since the late 1940s. Even much smaller Chile had a big steel mill in being, while Argentina's still remained on paper. In other respects as well, Argentina under Perón had lost its former position of economic leadership in Latin America, yielding first place in per capita income to Venezuela and in foreign trade to Brazil.

As its end drew near, the regime's economic failures still extended to vital aspects of the economy. By 1955 the deterioration of the railway system had gone so far that trains were running at half their normal speed. Just after Perón's fall, experts estimated that it would cost $1,200 million (U.S. currency) to rehabilitate them. The neglected national highways, it was found, needed a sum almost two thirds as large for their rehabilitation. Electric power shortages were severe. They first became a serious problem in Greater Buenos Aires in 1951 and four years later the supply fell nearly 30 per cent below the demand in this area, which accounted for seven tenths of the country's total consumption of electric power and an even larger proportion of its industrial production.

Similarly, production of petroleum by the government agency Y.P.F. fell further and further behind the mounting consumption of gasoline, fuel oil, and other petroleum products, thus necessitating larger imports and aggravating the balance of payments problem. Y.P.F.'s production, which had more than doubled in ten years under the oligarchy, 1930-40, increased only 20 per cent in nine years under Perón, while in these same nine years consumption grew 60 per cent. Yet Argentina's known petroleum resources were adequate to its needs if properly exploited, Y.P.F. had been in business since the 1920s, and Mexico and Bolivia, with similar agencies, were expanding production far more rapidly than Argentina and were even exporting to foreign countries. Why Perón failed to make a major effort in this case is hard to understand, especially since Y.P.F. had become a leading symbol of the national economic independence that he never tired of preaching. Perhaps the explanation lies in his faulty grasp of economics, or perhaps in the corruption and technical inefficiency that characterized his whole regime, and of which, by the early 1950s, Y.P.F. had become an outstanding exponent. At any rate, it was the heavy pressure of this petroleum problem that led Perón into one of the last and worst of his many errors, the Standard of California contract.

Totalitarianism Again

It may have been only a coincidence that the regime's years of economic depression after 1950 were marked by a resumption of the totalitarian drive heralded by Perón's speech of June 10, 1944, but later shunted aside or concealed during his pseudo-democratic period, which was also a prosperous period, from 1945 to 1949. But the connection between depression and totalitarian revival was probably causal rather than coincidental. As long as all was going well and Perón could be confident of getting what he wanted while paying lip service to the traditional institutions and practices of Argentine democracy, he had nothing to gain and much to lose by imposing an alien system of total control. This would only intensify an opposition which, though widespread, was being kept in its place very handily by less draconian methods.

When prosperity suddenly gave way to hard times, however, it was quite another story, for on the heels of hard times came political ferment. This was nothing new in Argentina: it had happened in 1890 and in 1930. Now it happened again. In 1951 disaffection appeared in both of the regime's main pillars, the descamisados and the military. Early in the year one of the oldest and strongest labor organizations in Argentina, a railway union, went on strike in defiance of government orders. In September came the first military revolt. Perón broke the strike and suppressed the revolt, but both were ominous signs.

The more serious of the two was, of course, the military revolt, and Perón responded to it with three measures. First, he seized absolute control of the armed forces. At his behest, a servile Congress empowered him to promote, demote, or retire officers at will. All that had been done in the last half century to professionalize Argentina's armed forces was now to be undone, and instead they were to be completely Peronized. In the second place, civilian controls were tightened by an act of Congress creating a new and more rigorous kind of martial law called the "state of internal war." Protests from the few Radical deputies during the *pro forma* debate on this measure elicited the tongue-in-cheek reply from its Peronist sponsors that "We cannot leave the democratic Justicialist state defenseless in the presence of its enemies." In the third place, a law was passed providing the death penalty for rebels.

This was only the beginning of a four-year-long process by which Perón sought to establish total control over every aspect of Argentine life by an apparatus of which he was the absolute master. As always, he sought to attain his objective gradually, by "successive turns of the screw," as he put it. After taking care (as he thought) of the military, he gave the screw another turn in the presidential campaign leading up to the election in November of this same year, 1951. While still maintaining the pretense of democracy, he reduced it to an indecent farce. The contrast with the substantially free and honest election that first brought him to office in 1946 was shocking, for now the opposition, represented only by the Radical party, was bullied, badgered, and denied the use of radio, press, and even posters. The only campaign instrument allowed it was political meetings, grudgingly licensed by Perón's police and frequently harassed or broken up by his rowdies. In these circumstances, the Radical candidates—Ricardo Balbín for president and Arturo Frondizi for vice president—did well to win one third of the total vote, which shot up to some 7,500,000, as this was the first national election in which women voted. Congress, now a near-monopoly of the Peronists, who won every seat in the Senate and all but a handful in the Chamber of Deputies, no longer made even a pretense of independence. On an almost unique occasion a senator had the audacity to oppose an administration measure and was promptly rewarded by expulsion. The servility of these representatives of a sovereign people plumbed new depths. The titles "Liberator of the Republic" and "Spiritual Chief of the Nation" were conferred on Perón and Eva, respectively, in May 1952, and in a single session the deputies rose reverently to their feet a hundred times when those august names were spoken.

The screw was given additional turns in 1952 and 1953 at the expense first of the Catholic Church and then of the universities. The former came as a byproduct of Eva Perón's death on July 26, 1952, which was followed by a week-long exhibition of such massive and emotional mourning as has seldom been seen anywhere in the world. The descamisados were not only the chief mourners; they also demanded, through one of their big labor unions, speaking for all, that Eva be canonized as Saint Eva of America. When this extraordinary proposal was coolly received, they charged the Church with hostility to their idol and some of them set on foot a movement to Peronize the Church and Christianity itself. Perón himself stood aloof from it at first and remained on apparently amicable terms with the Church until the very eve of his attack on it, which began late in 1954. In the meanwhile he completed the Peronization of the universities. A new law of December 1953 gave Perón a completely free hand in the appointment of deans as well as rectors, and required every university curriculum to include instruction in the "national doctrine," that is, Justicialism.

The grand climax began to develop in September 1954 with the opening of Perón's assault on the Catholic Church. This was no ordinary controversy over relations between Church and state. On the contrary, as Perón pressed forward in the next nine months from one position to another on an ever-broadening front, the Church-state issue took on the appearance of a mere pretext or occasion for a drive to establish totalitarian thought-control over every Argentine from the cradle to the grave, in religion as well as in education, in the primary and secondary schools as well as the universities, and in the armed forces as well as the civilian population. Hence it was that many Argentines who would never have taken up arms for the Catholic Church alone rallied to its defense in this crisis.

For several years before the assault began, there were signs in both parties to the Peronist-Church alliance of 1946 of a cooling toward each other. Yet Perón himself remained on the whole an apparently loyal son of the Church. Consequently, it came as a thunderclap when on September 29, 1954, he launched his campaign against it. This began with a speech in which he charged the Church with interfering in labor relations and trying to build up a separate political party—a reference to the nascent Christian Democratic party. Labor and politics, he asserted, were none of the Church's concern, and a separate party would necessarily be an opposition party. Made at a meeting with labor leaders, his speech was given little publicity, and for some time thereafter he left it to his henchmen and the controlled press to carry on the campaign. First alone, then with his open support, they pressed it with mounting violence until June 1955, when, frightened by a second military revolt, he brought the attack to a halt.

In the meanwhile, the government adopted a series of measures obviously designed not merely to put the Church in its place but to establish a universal system of thought control. First, by a succession of orders and decrees, beginning in November 1954, physical education in all primary and secondary schools, private as well as public, was placed under the control of the Ministry of Education. Secular "spiritual counselors" were appointed by the Eva Perón Foundation to advise students in such courses, which were made compulsory, and particularly to give the students "moral and spiritual orientation" in the national doctrine of Justicialism; and the bishops were deprived of the right to appoint instructors in catechism in the schools, which was transferred to, of all places, the government School Health Office. The law, based on a decree of 1943, making religious instructions compulsory was suspended on April 14, and repealed on June 1. The climax came in May, with the introduction in Congress of a bill to deprive the Church, and of course its schools, of tax exemption, and the passage of a measure calling a constitutional convention to consider the separation of Church and state. Barring a near-miracle, both measures were sure to be adopted.

In addition, the Church was now subjected to the general harassment with which the political parties of the opposition had long been familiar. Catholic radio broadcasts were prohibited and a Catholic newspaper and a Catholic publishing firm were closed down. Many priests and lay leaders of Catholic Action were arrested, and the latter were also dismissed from posts in the government and its numerous dependent institutions. The government even forbade newspapers to publish notices of Church services and other activities, and banks to extend credit to Catholic institutions. Crucifixes and images were removed from public offices, and the C.G.T. ordered them replaced with busts or portraits of the "Martyr of Labor," the late Eva Perón. Yet all the while Perón went on professing himself a devout Catholic. If one could believe him, he was only seeking to purify Argentine Catholicism. And following his divide-and-rule policy, he left all other religious denominations unmolested; according to census reports, they included less than 5 per cent of the total population of Argentina.

Winter of Military Discontent

With the press, radio, and television (established in 1951) already in his hands, and with the Church now, as he believed, cowed if not converted, it only remained for Perón to extend thought control to the armed forces. This he undertook to do by requiring them not only to take an oath of loyalty to the "national doctrine," which had become identified as a descamisado doctrine. This was bad enough, but they were also required to receive instruction in the doctrine, which was even worse. An order making the study of it obligatory in the navy, the service least loyal to the regime, is said to have sparked the long-planned revolt of June 1955.

Moreover, as the crisis unfolded, C.G.T. leaders redoubled the effort, begun years earlier, to give weapons and military training to the organized workers, now claimed (with some exaggeration) to number six million. This would of course break the military's monopoly of force and give Perón total control of the country, for the regime's other main pillar, regimented labor, was his own creation and submissive instrument. In short, the armed forces were now threatened with the completion of the process, begun in 1945, of whittling down the political power they had seized in 1943. By the same process, power was concentrated in the hands of Perón, whose populistic regime had become increasingly offensive to most of the officers on social and religious as well as political grounds.

It is no wonder, then, that a large part of the armed forces turned against Perón in this last phase of his drive for total control. Yet another large part of them remained loyal to him to the end, or at least did not rebel. Their loyalty is explained partly by the success of the efforts, mentioned earlier, to Peronize the sergeants. As for the officers, some were loyal to the regime because they held remunerative posts under it, some because they had become involved in corruption and feared exposure, and others because of personal ties with Perón.

Among the officers who rebelled, some, like General Eduardo Lonardi, were right-wing Catholics and worked closely with a civilian conspiratorial group of Catholic nationalists headed by Mario Amadeo. With the approval of the hierarchy, this group had supported Perón until the changing character of his regime completed their alienation. Now they spearheaded the conspiracy against him. But there were two other officer groups of at least equal importance. These were conservative democrats and liberal democrats, represented respectively by General Pedro Aramburu and Admiral Isaac Rojas. Both joined the Lonardi-Amadeo group in ousting Perón, but they were fundamentally antagonistic to it, and within another six weeks they ousted Lonardi and Amadeo too. In other words, Perón's final totalitarian drive provoked a resistance among the military as well as civilians which was far more than a Catholic reaction.

Perón no doubt failed to foresee the full strength of the resistance that this final turn of the screw would arouse. On the other hand he must have known that it would be stout and widespread. He surely knew that one of its centers of infection would be in the armed forces, which, first in October 1945 and again in September 1951, had been the source of the only serious threats to his hold on power that he had ever faced. And even if he had been completely lacking in foresight, once his campaign had been launched he could not have been blind to the evidence that it was provoking formidable resistance. Some of the evidence came from his secret service, which warned him that disaffection was spreading in the armed forces; he accordingly redoubled his security measures by transfers, retirements, and espionage. No secret service was needed to tell him that, despite harassment and even outright prohibition, mass meetings of the opposition were attracting twice as many people as those held by the C.G.T., despite all the help the latter received from Perón's police.

To be sure, the opposition drew its following almost exclusively from the middle and upper classes, but while the workers did not join it, they were no longer turning out *en masse* for demonstrations of loyalty to Perón. A May Day rally was held by the C.G.T. in the usual place, the Plaza de Mayo, but despite its best efforts to drum up attendance, only a paltry 50,000 descamisados assembled for the occasion, leaving the big plaza half empty. This was a sign of their cooling-off toward him since, in 1953, he had called a halt on handouts and told them that if they wanted higher wages, they must work harder and produce more, and had then compounded the offense by reversing his former attitude of hostility toward foreign investments and the United States. There is no evidence that any significant fraction of the descamisados had gone over to the opposition, but apparently a great many of them had lost their enthusiasm for the regime. So they gave Perón some of his own Third Position medicine, in the sense that they took a position of noncommitment as between him and the opposition.

Why, in the face of this situation—mounting resistance from the opposition, disquieting lethargy among the mass of his supporters —did Perón persist in his anticlerical, totalitarian campaign? The most plausible explanation is that it was designed to divert public attention from the economic depression, which was still deep when he launched the campaign, and also from a measure about to be adopted that was sure to be highly controversial: his contract with the Standard Oil Company of California. The contract had many merits from his point of view. Argentina's key problem was to increase domestic petroleum production and the United States was outstandingly well equipped to help solve it. Its solution would contribute greatly to the solution of another major problem, the balance of trade deficit. Finally, by signing the contract, he not only obtained a loan from the U.S. Export-Import Bank for the construction (at last!) of the coveted steel mill but also took an attitude which, he believed, would attract to Argentina a substantial portion of the investment capital that was then flowing in large volume from the United States to other Latin American countries. Once all this was accomplished, Argentina's economic troubles would be at an end and Perón would have plain sailing from then on. That was his expectation, and Washington's as well, but it proved to be built on sand.

Unfortunately for Perón, these benefits meant nothing to the host of Argentines who reacted violently against the contract as a betrayal of his own principles of economic independence and as a sell-out to Yankee imperialism. This may be why, in May and early June of 1955, shortly after news of the proposed contract became public property, he intensified his anticlerical campaign. If his purpose was to divert fire from the contract by stirring up trouble in another quarter, he succeeded only too well, for the result was a series of the worst disturbances of public order Buenos Aires had seen since his own brief ouster and triumphal return in October 1945.

The climax came in the week ending June 16, as Argentina's winter closed in. In quick succession, Catholics and non-Catholics made the feast of Corpus Christi the occasion for a mass meeting of protest in defiance of police orders; Peronists accused them of burning the Argentine flag and Perón expelled two Catholic prelates, shipping them off to Rome by airplane; whereupon, on June 16, the Vatican issued a decree of excommunication against all Argentines who had taken part in their expulsion. This included Perón and all his cabinet ministers.

That same day, though before news of the excommunication became generally known, the second military revolt against Perón took place in Buenos Aires. Though formidable, it was suppressed the same day, for everything went wrong for the rebels, beginning with the weather. That night, Peronist thugs, with government aid, retaliated by sacking and burning a dozen churches in the heart of the city.

Yet Perón was so shaken by the revolt that he embarked on an erratic course, marked first by retreat, then by overcompensating violence, and finally by indecision, which led to his ruin within less than a hundred days. In the first stage he tightened his security system, with the army's top general, Franklin Lucero, in charge; dropped his totalitarian, anticlerical campaign like a hot potato; and on July 5 delivered a most conciliatory radio address in which he pled with the opposition for "a political truce." Ten days later, as an earnest of good faith, he resigned the presidency of the Peronist party, proclaimed the end of his ten-year "revolution," and promised a prompt and full restoration of constitutional government. The opposition spokesmen, however, replied that they would not agree to a truce until Perón translated his fair words into "concrete measures," which they specified.

Unwilling to meet their terms, and informed by his secret service that a new military plot against him was afoot, Perón resumed the offensive with redoubled violence. Its resumption was signalized by the arrest of hundreds of his political opponents on August 15. A strong-arm gang one thousand strong, headed by one Guillermo Patricio Kelly, renegade son of an upper-class family, set about terrorizing the opposition. Perón himself brought the campaign of terror to its climax by threatening to unleash the whole descamisado horde. At a Peronist mass meeting in the Plaza de Mayo on August 31, he and his henchmen tried to stage "another October 17," as in 1945. This time, however, his speech was not a paean of victory but a call to battle. It was in fact the most incendiary speech he had ever made. After telling the descamisados to "annihilate and crush" those who would deprive them of the social gains made under his leadership, he continued:

> From now on . . . he who in any place tries to disturb order in opposition to constituted authorities or contrary to the law or the constitution may be slain by any Argentine. . . . And when one of our people falls, five of them will fall.

The armed forces, however, called a halt on this swing to the descamisados. When on September 7 the C.G.T. called for the arming of its six million members as a civilian militia, the proposal was promptly rejected by the Minister of War, General Franklin Lucero. Instead, Lucero intensified his purge of anti-Peronists in the armed forces.

Rather than let the government go on chewing up their rebel movement piecemeal, the conspirators started the revolt on September 16. It succeeded in three days. This third revolt against Perón, unlike the first two, started in the interior; it was also fought there and, in effect, won there, so that Perón's career resembled that of Rosas in yet another way: both, though holding the nation's metropolis, Buenos Aires, were defeated from the interior. It was a remarkable revolt in two respects: the fighting never spread to Buenos Aires, and the civilian population took almost no part in it on either side, the chief exception being the valiant and indispensable cooperation of Catholic laymen with the rebel troops under General Lonardi in the crucial operations at Córdoba. Like Uriburu's revolt of 1930, this was the armed forces' show. The last act was the threat of the rebel fleet under Admiral Rojas to bombard Buenos Aires, which lay within easy reach of its guns.

The threat did not need to be carried out, for the surrender of Buenos Aires came within twenty-four hours, on September 19. That Perón himself did not make it bespoke not courage but the weakness and indecision he showed throughout this final crisis. Even after the rebel fleet arrived in front of Buenos Aires his position was still strong. Only the fleet disputed his control of a metropolitan area containing more than a quarter of the nation's population and a concentration of troops that outnumbered all the rebel forces combined. The troops in this area were still loyal to him, as were the descamisado masses; the rest of the civilian population of Buenos Aires had made no move against him, and throughout history many cities have borne up under far greater punishment than Rojas' fleet could have inflicted on it. Yet when Perón's generals advised him to yield, he did so without making any effort to call out the descamisados whom he had so recently incited to "kill five of the enemy for every one of us that falls." Much less did he keep his promise to fight for them to the end. When he was ready to quit, he gave a junta of his generals the responsibility of arranging the surrender. And when he fled to save his own hide, leaving his followers to shift for themselves, he bought his way out with a tricky "renunciation" which, as soon as he was safe on foreign soil, he claimed was not a resignation.

Rosas had fled from Argentina in a British ship. Perón first took refuge in a Paraguayan gunboat at Buenos Aires. Two weeks later he was flown in a hydroplane of the Paraguayan air force to Asunción, where his friend General Stroessner ruled.

Whose Tragedy?

Despite all his faults and failures, Perón made a great and lasting impact on Argentina. His principal achievement, and his only important one, was to better the lot of the Argentine workers, rural as well as urban, by giving them organization, better wages, social security and other fringe benefits, and, for the first time, a sense of dignity and of counting for something in Argentine public life. After his fall, the greater part of his revolution on their behalf proved irreversible and the "Peronist vote" became one of the principal prizes for which political leaders of the right as well as the center and left contended.

For the rest, Perón's role was negative when it was not pernicious. He revolutionized the implications of nationalism by identifying it with social revolution, but any good this might have done was cancelled out by the irrational, demagogic, xenophobe character of his nationalism. The claim that he industrialized Argentina has no basis in fact, for its industrialization had already been making rapid and substantial progress for a decade before he began his rise to power; otherwise he would never have come to power. In addition, his industrial program was so ill-conceived and so inefficiently and corruptly administered that, besides falling far short of what should have been achieved, it crippled the basic agricultural-pastoral economy. He inflicted heavy losses on the land-owning oligarchy, but did nothing to reform the agrarian system. The end result was economic stagnation in Argentina while other Latin American countries were advancing rapidly.

Other results of Perón's rule were social fragmentation and political degradation. His vaunted Justicialism was at best a useful political instrument; as a system of political thought it was pretentious nonsense. In the closing years of his regime he deserted his own principles, and at the very end he deserted his most faithful followers, the descamisados. If there is any element of tragedy in his career, the tragedy lies not in what happened to him but in what he did to Argentina: in his gross misuse of a golden opportunity for service to the nation while he was in power, and in the heritage of economic ruin, moral decay, and political and social chaos that he left behind him when he fled.

NINE

A HAUNTED HOUSE

1955-1963

At the present writing more than eight years have passed since Perón's fall and flight, and in all that time he has never set foot in Argentina again. Yet to the nation's constant distraction and almost to its undoing, his ghost has continued to haunt it in one of two incompatible images: one, as Perón the redeemer who could do no wrong; the other, as Perón the Beelzebub who could do nothing but wrong. Both were false, and this was understood by all reasonable Argentines, who were probably the majority. But they were overborne by extremists so strongly entrenched in rival power groups—the Peronists in organized labor, the anti-Peronists in the armed forces—that their intransigent hostility to each other kept the country in constant turmoil.

Perón's quick rehabilitation as the descamisados' redeemer may seem puzzling, since toward the end of his regime they had become disillusioned with him and failed to rally to his defense when he was ousted. The best explanation is the conservative character of the government that replaced his, for they soon came to regard it as the agent of a reaction in favor of the oligarchy and Yankee imperialism and as a threat to their "social conquests" under Perón and to Argentina's economic independence. So the Perón regime became their nostalgic *belle époque*, with Perón himself again, inevitably, their peerless leader. From various places of exile, finally Spain, he played the role vigorously with the aid of large funds he had salted away abroad. The result was to exacerbate the anti-Peronists and create an impasse from which there seemed to be no escape except by armed force. It was this conflict that wrecked the well-intentioned efforts at pacification and economic recovery made by constitutional President Arturo Frondizi from 1958 to 1962 and led to his ouster early in the latter year. For a time the strife was only intensified, but at last in mid-1963 came the first faint but hopeful sign of peace.

The Liberating Revolution

The first provisional government set up by the leaders of the Liberating Revolution on the ruins of the Perón regime was headed by General Eduardo Lonardi as Provisional President and Admiral Isaac Rojas as Provisional Vice President. Lonardi chose as his motto the time-honored Argentine phrase, "neither victors nor vanquished" (*ni vencedores ni vencidos*). Used by Urquiza after Rosas' overthrow in 1852, the phrase expressed the spirit of compromise which had prevailed in the framing of Argentina's Constitution of 1853. It also had an analogy in the spirit of national reconciliation that characterized the attitudes of both General Grant and President Lincoln toward the South at the close of our Civil War.

This policy was one of the main reasons why Lonardi lasted less than two months as Provisional President. There had been no agreement on policy among the diverse elements that overthrew Perón, and many of the victors thought Lonardi was entirely too easy on the vanquished Peronists, both in the armed forces and in labor; he even left them in possession of their citadel, the C.G.T. He also offended many by showing too much favor to right-wing Catholics, one of whom, Mario Amadeo, was his chief lieutenant.

Both issues were given headline billing in a radio address on November 3 by a Radical leader, Ernesto Enrique Sammartino, who, warning that the Liberating Revolution was facing serious threats from two counterrevolutionary forces, continued:

> One of these forces is represented by the remains of the overthrown regime, the C.G.T. and . . . the political organizations of Peronism. . . . The second conspiracy . . . is that nourished by reactionary forces of dogmatic and fascist mentality. This second counterrevolution, that of Argentina's medieval period, is more dangerous than the first. It has its black popes and its brown-shirted strategists.

On these and other grounds Lonardi was forced out by a group of his fellow officers on November 13, after only eight weeks in office.

Brief though his tenure was, Lonardi left an enduring imprint in three ways. First, his policy of national reconciliation was revived by President Arturo Frondizi in 1958. Second, in order to palliate the dictatorial character of his regime, he established a civilian National Consultative Council, consisting of 20 representatives of all the political parties except the Communists and the Peronists; this was continued by his successor, General Pedro Aramburu. So also was Lonardi's use of Raúl Prebisch as economic adviser. Former head of Argentina's Central Bank and an exile of the Perón period, and at this time chairman of the Economic Commission for Latin America (ECLA), a United Nations body, Prebisch promptly filed a report describing the "disastrous" economic situation inherited from Perón, and followed this up with a plan for recovery and development which recommended austerity, free enterprise, and the encouragement of foreign investments.

Dictatorship for Democracy: Aramburu

After Lonardi's removal power was vested in a five-man junta which ruled Argentina for the next two and a half years, until the restoration of civilian government on May 1, 1958. It was headed throughout by General Aramburu, as Provisional President, and Admiral Rojas, who stayed on as Provisional Vice President. The other members were the chiefs of the army, navy, and air force. Such voice as civilians had was provided by the National Consultative Council; but this was only an advisory body. Decision-making was the exclusive province of the military junta, which ruled by decree. There was no Congress; Perón's had been dissolved by Lonardi and a new one was not elected until 1958. There was a Supreme Court, but this body, having been purged of Peronism and reconstituted by Lonardi in the spirit of the Liberating Revolution, gave the junta no trouble.

Aramburu desperately needed all the power he could get, for his first seven months in office were dominated by his struggle to maintain his Provisional Government against a mounting tide of opposition. This came from many quarters including the military as well as civilians, and Catholic nationalist adherents of Lonardi as well as descamisado devotees of Perón. Interspersed with sabotage, bombings, strikes, and conspiracies, this seven-month period was bracketed by the two greatest threats to the regime: a revolutionary general strike by the C.G.T. in November 1955 and a military revolt in June 1956. Aramburu suppressed both with exemplary rigor and, in the interval between them, pushed ahead at high speed with his de-Peronization program.

In breaking the C.G.T. strike Aramburu made full use of the police and the armed forces, stopped the strikers' pay, and arrested several hundred labor leaders, half of whom were kept in jail for the next six months. His task was made easier by the refusal of the "independent" unions, about one third of the total, to support the strike; labor, too, was divided. As soon as the strike had been broken he "intervened" the C.G.T. and its component unions, that is, placed them under government administrators; the intervention continued until 1961. Characteristically, he chose a naval captain for the principal post, interventor of the C.G.T. Next, he concentrated on de-Peronization, which he applied to business firms as well as politicians and the military. Interventors were placed in charge of some 300 firms, large and small, individual and corporate. The men's and women's Peronist parties were outlawed. All Peronist officeholders, from Perón and his cabinet ministers down to village mayors, were barred from office, not only in the government but in any political party, and their bank accounts and other records were investigated for evidences of corruption. Greatly intensifying the armed forces purge begun by Lonardi, Aramburu dismissed or retired, and in some cases imprisoned, dozens of generals, scores of officers of lower rank, and an unknown number of noncommissioned officers.

These stern measures helped to spark the military revolt of June 9-10, which was the work of Catholic nationalists as well as Peronists among the officer corps. If successful in the early stages, it would have been supported by civilians of both groups. Instead, it was quickly snuffed out; and as a warning, 27 of the ringleaders, including a general, were summarily court-martialled and shot. This was something that even Perón had never done to military rebels. His new law of 1951 legalized such action, but it violated a clause of the restored Constitution of 1853 which prohibited the death penalty for political crimes. Nevertheless, it apparently had the desired effect. At any rate, from this time on, Aramburu's hold was never again seriously threatened until he relinquished it voluntarily nearly two years later.

Although the military junta was in effect the judge of its own powers, it recognized the supremacy of the Constitution and promised, in Aramburu's words, to "re-establish the reign of law and return the country to genuine democracy." In short, the junta was only a caretaker government. Again, as in 1930 and 1943, the Supreme Court obligingly accepted this view and accorded the military dictatorship *de facto* recognition.

But which constitution was to prevail? That of 1853? Or Perón's revised version of 1949, which had been adopted by a duly elected convention? This was an embarrassing question which it took several months to answer. When the answer came, it showed how elastic the concept of caretaker government could be: on May 1, 1956, Provisional President Aramburu simply cancelled Perón's constitution by decree, at the same time restoring the one of 1853 to full force and effect (except as suspended by the junta). From time to time the junta stepped out of its caretaker role. An example is the celebrated case of the newspaper *La Prensa*, which had been seized under Perón. In this case the junta cut short the judicial proceedings required by Lonardi and restored the newspaper to its owners by decree.

Considering the circumstances, however, General Aramburu carried out his political pledge with a high degree of fidelity and success. He was one of the many officers who had served Perón with apparent loyalty for years, had thereby provided Peronism with one of its two main pillars, and had turned against it just in time to be identified with the Liberating Revolution. But he was also one of the smaller but still considerable number of officers in whom the bitter experience with Peronism had produced a revulsion in favor of returning the country to constitutional democracy and the armed forces to their traditional nonpolitical role. Neither politically nor socially was he a second Uriburu, much less a second Perón, and his two and a half years as the guiding force in a military dictatorship came to a fitting close when he procured the peaceful inauguration of a highly controversial president, Arturo Frondizi, whose election he and most of his fellow officers deplored.

One factor in the situation greatly favored Aramburu: the Argentine economy made a quick recovery during his years in office.* It was to take much longer to repair all the damage done by Perón, but, happily for Aramburu, the terms of trade took a more favorable turn just at this time. A small but particularly gratifying contribution to the improvement came from the rapid rise of exports of Argentine boned beef to the United States. The small amount of such shipments was doubled in the next two years and then increased fivefold in 1958, when their value exceeded $29 million. What made the increase so gratifying was that it signified a sizeable breach in the wall of exclusion raised against Argentine beef by the United States government's sanitary embargo of 1927. In May 1959 Washington closed the breach by a new sanitary order, and so wiped out this transient new market for Argentine beef, but that was a year after Aramburu went out of office.

Yet, at the end of his dictatorship of two-and-a-half years, Aramburu was still so far from completing his task and the nation was so deeply divided in so many ways that one may wonder whether his de-Peronization policy had worked any better than Lonardi's national reconciliation might have done. Aramburu's lack of success even in his own special province, the military, became glaringly apparent almost as soon as his strong hand was removed. Despite his elimination of two dissident officer groups, Peronists and Catholic nationalists, there remained another group who complained that his anti-Peronist campaign was not conducted either with sufficient thoroughness or on a broad enough front. Among the latter was his own vice president, Admiral Rojas. He failed to get the military out of politics; some think he weakened their morale as well as their technical efficiency by repeated purges; and yet even so there remained a strong dissident group, the hard-boiled extremists appropriately called "gorillas," who complained that even he was too easy on the Peronists.

Resentment was keenest among the workers. They noted that

* On the other hand, Aramburu's failure to cut back unessential imports forced his successor, Frondizi, to take that unpopular step at once because of the large balance of trade deficit inherited from Aramburu.

Aramburu's advisers on economic questions included representatives of business but not of labor. They rejected the whole Prebisch approach to these questions, but particularly galling to them was the operation of the wage controls instituted late in 1955. These were applied in a way that was supposed to compensate the workers for price increases resulting from the devaluation of the peso, but they failed to do so, and the workers were soon complaining that while wages walked upstairs, prices shot up in the elevator. Other grievances abounded, including the government's intervention in the labor unions. So it was easy for labor leaders to convince most of the rank and file that the anti-Peronist campaign was in reality part of a plot to restore the old corrupt alliance between the Argentine oligarchy and foreign economic imperialists and to rob the workers of their "social conquests." Hence the quick rehabilitation of Perón as the workers' patron saint.

Civilian Rule Restored: Frondizi

Perhaps unwittingly, the outstanding Radical leader of this period, Arturo Frondizi, contributed to the reinvigoration of Peronism among the workers. Even before 1955, when Frondizi was a leading opponent of the Perón regime, he and his fellow Radicals had vied with Perón in bidding for labor support and had reinforced their bid with verbal assaults on the Argentine oligarchy, foreign economic imperialism, and the "corrupt alliance" between the two. In fact, the positions of the two men coincided at so many points that one is tempted to say that after September 1955 Frondizi himself was the best representative of "Peronism without Perón." In the final crisis of 1955, he hoisted Perón with his own petard of economic nationalism by leading a savage attack on the latter's Standard Oil contract as a sell-out to Yankee imperialism. As soon as Perón was ousted, Frondizi and his cohorts launched an almost frantic campaign to win the Peronist vote with promises to protect the workers' "social conquests" against the oligarchy and foreign imperialists and to bring about a complete transformation of Argentine society.

Frondizi soon emerged as the principal contender for the presidency in the election of February 1958. The Radical Party, reunited in the Perón period, split again, early in 1957, into two quite separate parties. Both retained the historic original name, Unión Cívica

Radical, and added an identifying tag. Frondizi's chose "Intransigent" and so became known as the UCRI. The other wing retaliated by adopting the suffix "del Pueblo" ("of the People"), and is referred to as the People's or Popular Radicals. Its candidate was Ricardo Balbín, who had headed the ticket of a united Radical Party in 1951, with Frondizi in second place. Now the two men were bitter rivals, and their personal rivalry was mainly responsible for the party schism.

These two Radical parties were the largest legal parties, and one of them was sure to win the election, but since each controlled only about one fourth of the votes, the equally numerous Peronists, whose party was still outlawed, held the balance of power between them. Through a deal with Perón, Frondizi realized his dream of winning this big bloc of votes, thus assuring his election. For good measure, he also received the support of the Communists (estimated to number about 70,000) and their fellow-travellers. As a result, he garnered two thirds of the popular vote and an even larger share of the electoral vote, and his party won control of both houses of Congress by similar margins. Except for Perón's rigged election of 1951, it was the greatest victory any political leader in Argentina had won since Irigoyen's walkover in 1928. But the parallel was an ominous one in view of what had happened to Irigoyen in 1930.

The omens for Frondizi were not much better if one took a realistic view of his situation on the morrow of his triumph. He had won through an alliance with a Peronist bloc which was at least as large as his own Intransigent Radical Party, was at least as well disciplined, and took its orders not from him but from the exiled Perón. That he had won with Peronist and Communist aid intensified the hostility to him engendered among all moderate and right-wing elements by his demagogic campaign. Unfortunately for him, such hostility was most pronounced among the military. And finally, the only other large party to which he might have looked for help, the People's Radicals, were embittered against him for having, as they charged, split the Radical Party and betrayed his former chief, Balbín, to serve his own personal ambition. As it proved, that split was a national disaster.

Despite persistent rumors of an impending military coup of anti-

Peronist officers who detested Frondizi, he was duly inaugurated on May 1, 1958. Thanks to the military junta's control of the armed forces, it was able to keep its promise to restore the government to the civilians. Such an event was rare in the history of Latin America, but before many months had passed it turned out that many of the Argentine military still regarded themselves as the final arbiter of its political disputes.

Frondizi's inaugural address dealt almost wholly with foreign policy—as was fitting, since the audience contained many foreign dignitaries, among them Vice President Richard Nixon, who was starting on his ill-fated tour of South America. Nationalism ran like a scarlet thread through the address, but it was braided with internationalism which, Frondizi promised, would characterize his foreign policy. Thus, after advocating a policy of "complete identification" of Argentina with "the sister countries of Latin America" aimed at promoting "the economic development and integration of each one of these countries," he explained:

> In order that Latin America may become a powerful community of nations, it is indispensable that each one of them attain the greatest prosperity possible, since the development of each Latin American nation will make it possible to accelerate the development of the rest.

Latin America was given top priority in this brief address. The United States was not mentioned once by name, and the only clear reference to it occurred in a passage in which Frondizi complained of the painfully manifest inequality between "the progress and well-being achieved in one part of America, and the backwardness and misery in which millions of people live submerged in the other part of America, our America." Only when this inequality had been corrected, he continued, would true continental unity become possible. "Historically," he said, Argentina belonged to "the cultural world of the West" but "ought to trade with all nations of the earth, without distinction." His cool statement that Argentina should "remain in the Organization of American States" contrasted with his unqualified assertion that "the solution of all problems of an international character should be discussed and reached in the United Nations" and its subsidiary organizations. His enumeration of the basic principles of Argentine foreign policy built up to the "self-determination and complete sovereignty of all nations on a footing of absolute equality."

In the main, he adhered to the foreign policy laid down in this address until another military coup ousted him from office just short of four years later. Throughout, he maintained the strong stress laid on foreign policy in his inaugural. This was illustrated by his many trips abroad; he was by far the most peripatetic president Argentina had ever had. His travels took him to other Latin American countries, the United States, Europe, and even to India. His objectives were mainly, but by no means exclusively, economic. In the United States and Europe he sought support from private investors, national governments, and international agencies. In Europe another major objective was to protect Argentina, along with other Latin American countries, against the threat from the European Common Market to their agricultural exports. In Latin America, spurred by the Common Market and other examples of Old World cooperation, his government joined Brazil, Chile, Mexico, Uruguay, Paraguay, and Peru in forming the Latin American Free Trade Association (1960) for lowering trade barriers.

One important policy development not hinted at in his inaugural was the formation of a special relationship with the United States. Previously, his ardent nationalism had caused him to be regarded in some circles as a Yankeephobe, but during his presidency relations between the U.S. and Argentina became friendlier and more cooperative than at any time since the administration of Sarmiento, whose motto had been, "Argentina must North Americanize herself." Even their policy clash over Castro's Cuba, of which more will be said below, did not destroy the entente. Until the very eve of his overthrow in 1962, Frondizi was still receiving fresh financial aid from Washington, and the latter was still hoping to make Argentina, with his cooperation, a showcase for the Alliance for Progress.

Though Frondizi's reasons for forming this strange friendship are not yet fully known, the chief reason seems quite clear: he had ambitious plans for economic development which could not be carried out without help from the United States. The Soviet Union had by this time launched a foreign aid program and he involved Argentina in it on a relatively small scale; but that was probably as far as he wanted to go on the road to Moscow, and he knew that the armed forces and others in Argentina would not tolerate his going any further. Even his rapprochement with the United States offended powerful nationalist groups; in relations with the Soviet bloc, nationalist susceptibilities were reinforced by hostility to Communism, although since Perón's rise Argentina's Communists have never had enough strength to be more than a nuisance.

Upset by Stabilization

Three measures adopted by Frondizi in his first eight months in office alienated most of the left-wing voters and other nationalists who had swelled his big majority in the presidential election. First, in July 1958, he began to enter into a series of contracts with foreign firms, mainly in the United States, though also in Europe, for the exploitation of Argentina's petroleum resources. This provocative policy, carried out by decrees whose legality was contested, recalled the Standard Oil of California contract that had contributed mightily to Perón's undoing. The opposition was not appeased by Frondizi's assurances that the terms of his contracts safeguarded Argentina's national interests, including specifically those of Y.P.F., and that this use of foreign firms would help greatly in the achievement of Argentina's economic independence by converting it from a heavy importer into an exporter of petroleum products. The second measure, adopted in September, was a law which gave degrees granted by Catholic and other private educational institutions equal validity with those granted by public institutions. Though presented in the name of freedom (*libre enseñanza* was the label), the new law was strongly reprobated by most liberals as contrary to Argentina's long-established tradition of secular education.

Most controversial of all was the Stabilization Agreement of December 1958 with the International Monetary Fund, under encouragement from the United States and with a promise of its assistance. Much more far-reaching than its name indicated, this was the basis of a plan for long-range economic development as well as stabilization, and it involved international commitments to free enterprise, the encouragement of foreign capital investments, and a regime of austerity. In most respects the agreement conflicted with Frondizi's promises in the presidential campaign. It was hotly opposed both by many nationalists and especially by the workers, who were convinced that they would be forced to bear the main burden of austerity. Since two thirds of these workers were Peronists, Frondizi was caught in a dilemma, for throughout his administration it was his political policy to conciliate the Peronists and yet his economic policy alienated them. Moreover, it provoked them to a course of violent opposition that called forth an equal and opposite reaction on the part of anti-Peronists. In this sense, the Stabilization Plan had much to do with keeping the country in a state of highly unstable equilibrium until Frondizi's government came crashing down in 1962.

Theoretically, a strong case can be made in favor of Frondizi's new policy. There are only three ways in which an underdeveloped country, or (as in the case of Argentina) one in the intermediate stage of development, can expand its economy rapidly. The first two are based wholly on forced savings imposed on the masses: in one case, under state management by an authoritarian regime, as in the Soviet Union; in the other, under a free enterprise system in which the government keeps the masses in their place while an elite accumulates and reinvests capital, as in the England of the Industrial Revolution. Since both of these methods were unthinkable in Argentina at this time, Frondizi perforce tried the third, which was the massive employment of foreign capital under a system of free enterprise with a minimum of government controls.

Such a system had worked well in the United States in the nineteenth century, and its example appears to have weighed heavily with Frondizi. Unfortunately for him, the situation facing him in Argentina bore little resemblance to the one in the nineteenth-century United States. Argentina was now deeply fragmented, both politically and socially, and great masses of its people had developed a deep-seated and largely unreasoning hostility to private enterprise and the capitalist system. They were also too impatient to enlarge their "social conquests" to accept the fact that, in a developing country, economic growth must be given precedence over social reforms, as Frondizi now proposed to do. As it happened, these were the people whose votes had been largely responsible for his election.

Two results of the great popular resentment aroused by Frondizi's new economic policy should be noted. One was a political disaster. His chances of winning the workers over to his Intransigent Radical

Party all but vanished. The great bulk of them remained so obedient to Perón that when their absentee leader, who by this time was living in Spain, ordered them to cast blank ballots in the election of 1960, some two million of them did so, turning it into a rout for Frondizi. His party's share of the votes amounted to only one fourth of the total, which was equalled by the People's Radical Party and exceeded by the Peronist bloc of blank ballots. Nearly all the remaining votes were cast for minor parties opposed to Frondizi, who was now a minority president with a vengeance: three voters in every four had declared against him. This proportion remained substantially unaltered to the end of his tenure. The second result was the outbreak of a sustained rash of strikes, sabotage, and bombings. These were attributed, no doubt correctly, to agents of Communism and (after 1959) of Cuban Castroism as well as to the Peronists, but they were symptoms of deep discontent among the masses. They maintained a sense of tension and insecurity, impeded Frondizi's efforts at financial stabilization and economic development, and provoked strong reactions in other sectors of society.

Soldiers' Return

The strongest reaction took place among the military. Many of them had accepted Frondizi as president on sufferance and kept looking for a chance to get rid of him. Yet, for lack of strong civilian support of his government, its very existence depended on the military. As a concession to them, he reluctantly accepted the "Conintes Plan," under which the campaign of violence was combatted by empowering military courts to mete out summary justice in cases involving crimes against the security of the state.

And yet in his eagerness to wean the workers away from Perón, and his invincible optimism that he could do the job, Frondizi continued to irritate the military over the issue of Peronism even in minor matters. An example is the case of Rogelio Frigerio, a self-made man of means, whom many of the military detested as the leading pro-Peronist in Frondizi's entourage: to placate them Frigerio was dropped as an official only to return through the back door as a member of the kitchen cabinet. Still worse from the military point of view was the termination of the last government controls over the C.G.T., which was returned to the worker in 1961, with the result that the Peronists tightened their hold on this key organization. According to one count, there were 34 attempted coups or major crises of one kind or another during Frondizi's tenure, and most of these were the work of the military extremists. As always, however, the armed forces were politically divided. Some of them, still best represented by Aramburu, supported the government, mainly on the ground that, however bad Frondizi might be, another overthrow of constitutional democracy would be still worse, and Argentina would become indistinguishable from the perpetually unstable "banana republics" of the Caribbean on which Argentines had always looked down with contempt. As time went on, however, the hold of these moderates over their more impatient military colleagues became weaker and weaker, until early in 1962 it was broken.

The final crisis began when Frondizi took a soft line on the problem of Castro's Cuba at the meeting of American foreign ministers at Punta del Este, Uruguay, in January 1962. Argentina, one of the few American states that still maintained diplomatic relations with Cuba, opposed the key measure, the expulsion of Castro's government from the Inter-American System. Both during and after the Punta del Este meeting, the Argentine military protested vehemently against the position taken by their government there. On February 3, Frondizi countered with what sounded like a fighting speech broadcast from Paraná, pledging "my honor and my life" to the "total defense" of his principles. But the Argentine people's response to his call was so uncertain that, despite his brave words, he soon yielded to the extent of severing diplomatic relations with Cuba. That, as it turned out, only won his government a stay of execution.

Changing Guard

The melodrama moved to a quick conclusion after Frondizi let the Peronists present their own candidates in the national election of March 1962, for the first time since Perón's fall. Why he did so remains a puzzle. His action has been ascribed to a statesmanlike devotion to the principle of national reconciliation; but statesmanship requires good timing, and it would have been hard to find a less propitious time for this most controversial step. A more plausible explanation is that Frondizi was overconfident because of recent victories by his Intransigent Radical Party in three provincial elections. At any rate, it seems clear that this once shrewd political analyst had lost touch with public opinion through pressure of affairs of state, and that the advisers who should have kept him in touch with it were incredibly mistaken in their estimates. These could not be corrected by public opinion polls, and the Argentine newspapers were of little use for this purpose: when they did not merely reflect the opinions of those who footed their bills, they provided at best a rough indication of the preferences of the small fragment of the nation's population that each served.

However justifiable the error may have been, it was egregious, for the Peronists won the election by a wide margin. Campaigning under different labels in different provinces ("Justicialist" was one of the favorites), they polled a popular vote nearly 40 per cent larger than that of the second party, Frondizi's Intransigent Radicals, who came in just ahead of the People's Radicals; the remainder of the vote was scattered among Socialists, Christian Democrats (who in some provinces voted with the Peronists), and a dozen other parties. The Peronists' popular vote was only 35 per cent of the total, but under the Saenz Peña Law, which required only a plurality, this was enough to give them control of ten provinces, including the largest of all, the Province of Buenos Aires. It also gave them a substantial minority of 46 seats in the Chamber of Deputies and assurance of strong representation in the Senate once their newly elected provincial governments were installed.

Seeking to forestall a counterstroke from the anti-Peronist military, leading Peronists hastened to make conciliatory, reassuring gestures. One of them, Andrés Framini, just elected governor of the Province of Buenos Aires and long the head of the strong Textile Workers Union, immediately held press conferences in which he stressed the "Christian, humane, Western, Argentine," character of Peronism, disowned ties or sympathy with "foreign ideologies," and affirmed that private enterprise and capitalism would be fully respected. The very next morning, as a warranty of his Christian sentiments, Framini sought and obtained a well-publicized audience with Cardinal-Archbishop Caggiano of Buenos Aires.

All this was to no avail. The military put heavy pressure on Frondizi to upset the results of the election by decreeing intervention in all ten of the provinces won by the Peronists. After a brief resistance he gave in to the extent of intervening in the five in which they had won without the aid of other parties; among these was the key province of Buenos Aires. This surrender not only gravely compromised his moral and political authority, but also soon proved fruitless. Nevertheless, the denunciation with which it was greeted by liberals in the United States and elsewhere was excessive on at least two grounds. It did not, as alleged, defeat the will of the Argentine people. Only 35 per cent of them had voted for the Peronist tickets; the remaining 65 per cent had voted for other parties, all of which were anti-Peronist. Nor did the intervention violate Argentina's Constitution, as many charged. That Constitution explicitly gives the Federal government the right to intervene in the provinces for various purposes, including protection of the republican form of government; many presidents of Argentina have used this power for political purposes, just as Frondizi did on this occasion; and Argentina's Supreme Court has uniformly refused to review the constitutionality of their acts, on the ground that these are political questions and, as such, not within the court's jurisdiction.

Frondizi's surrender to the militant military in the matter of intervention did not save him. They were determined not to leave this bungler (as they called him in their more charitable moments) in control as before. Instead, they insisted that he renovate his government by forming a kind of coalition, a ministry of all the democratic talents. This he was unable to do, for now the chickens came home to roost: the only other large democratic party besides his own was the Popular Radicals; without them no coalition worthy of the name could be formed; but, embittered by Frondizi's splitting of the Radical Party in 1957 and his high-handed treatment of them since then, they would have nothing to do with any coalition of which he was a part. Most of the smaller parties likewise refused. Many of their leaders had nothing but harsh things to say about him. "Machiavellian," "double-dealing," and "disruptive" were their favorite epithets. If these civilian political leaders could be believed, Frondizi and the coterie around him were more to blame than the military, the Peronists, or anyone else for the sorry pass to which Argentina had been brought.

They did Frondizi a grave injustice. Whatever his faults in timing and other respects, he had offered the country wise solutions for its two major problems: for its limping economy, his stabilization and development plan; for its basic political and social problem, Peronism, restoration of the Peronist masses to first-class citizenship. It was his misfortune, and the country's, that these problems were so intertwined that each contributed to frustrating the solution of the other, and that at the end of his four years in office little had been gained in either respect and much lost in both.

On March 30, 1962, the military turned Frondizi out. When he refused to resign, they arrested him and sent him to the Island of Martín García in the Plata estuary. The same thing had been done with Perón in 1945, but there the brief parallel ended, for Frondizi had no triumphal return to power. After several months he was transferred to Bariloche, a pleasant vacation spot amid lakes and woods in Argentina's Andean foothills, where distinguished visitors from the United States and other countries have been entertained. For Frondizi, however, it was a prison, and he was not released until after another constitutional president had at last been elected in July 1963.

In the meanwhile the country had been governed by a nominally civilian regime which was in effect another military dictatorship, and had passed through another series of crises and conflicts verging on civil war. War might have broken out if Argentine society had been simply bifurcated. Instead, it was split into many fragments which not even the issue of Peronism could polarize. Both Peronists and anti-Peronists quarrelled among themselves. Thus, the nearest approach to civil war came in September 1962 when two military factions, the Reds and the Blues, both anti-Peronist, fought each other for control of the government. Aside from personalities, the main question at issue between them was whether to take a hard, dictatorial line against the Peronists, as advocated by the Reds or neogorillas, or a more moderate and constitutional line, as urged by the Blues. Fortunately for the peace of Argentina, the Blues won, and, though after many more trials and tribulations, the promised election was duly held and a constitutional government once more took office on October 12, 1963.

The new president, Arturo Illia, a Popular Radical, was a 63-year-old physician who for many years had practiced medicine and politics in a small town in the province of Córdoba. Though a worthy man and a party wheelhorse, he was almost as colorless as the José Tamborini defeated by Perón in 1946. It was a hopeful sign that such a man could win now, for it might mean that the Argentines had had enough of heroics and contention and were in a mood to get the country moving again after a stagnation that had lasted with little interruption for more than a dozen years. It was good, too, that the new president was a provincial, for none had been elected since the turn of the century. It was a still better augury that his election was apparently welcomed with relief by most Argentines, whether they had voted for him or not; once the election was over, reported one observer, "they turned their attention to a full slate of major-league soccer matches, the national pastime, and to horse racing."

Prospects for a relaxation of political tensions improved as a result of the reverses suffered by Frondizi and Perón in this election. They had joined forces again for the occasion, first in promoting a coalition and then, when that was outlawed, in calling on their followers to cast blank ballots, but about half of them refused to do so, some Peronists voting for Illia, and Frondizi's party splitting again. Neither man was by any means done for, but their capacity for harassing the new government had been reduced and the country's new mood seemed likely to reduce it still further.

The new government had its work cut out for it. Steep price inflation, the flight of private capital, heavy unemployment, unfavorable terms of trade, a snow-balling foreign debt, and the threat from the European Common Market presented some of the more pressing problems. There was also the cluster of still unsettled social problems produced a generation or more earlier by rapid economic development and the attendant growth of social complexity. To make matters worse, the handicap imposed on the government by political fragmentation was aggravated by the shift in 1963 from the Saenz Peña Law to proportional representation.*

President Illia gave two early clues to his plans for achieving domestic peace and recovery. First, while he sought to extradite Perón from Spain, he eased restrictions on the Peronists in Argentina. Second, he cancelled Frondizi's petroleum contracts with foreign companies. Since the latter measure was regarded as a challenge to the United States, one might assume that the new government intended

* See Chapter One.

to employ the familiar device of distracting giddy minds from troubles at home by stirring up foreign quarrels. The challenge was tempered, however, by Illia's kind words in his inaugural address for the Alliance for Progress, which the United States gave first place in its Latin American policy and of which Argentina, as a still developing nation, stood in need.

The longer-range outlook was still dominated by the peculiarly Argentine phenomenon of Peronism. The armed forces, which had first helped summon forth that genie and then had led the fight to bottle it up again, gave some indication that they were at last ready to return to their barracks and leave the solution of political problems to the constitutional civilian government. This was one evidence of the striking capacity for survival demonstrated by Argentina's democratic tradition through more than three decades of extraordinary stress and change both at home and in that outside world to which so many Argentines have always been closely attuned. Given the character of the people and their country, there was reason to hope that it was a capacity not only for survival but for renewed growth.

```
┌─────────────────────────────────────┐
│                                       │
│         SUGGESTED READINGS            │
│                                       │
│                                       │
└─────────────────────────────────────┘
```

The literature dealing with Argentina's development in the national period is very abundant and scarcely less controversial. The latter feature, though present from the start, has been greatly accentuated since the turn of the century, probably as a result of tensions that first arose from the transformation of Argentine society described in the text. An early illustration involves the identification of the basic conflict in the nation's life. In his mid-nineteenth-century classic *Facundo*, Domingo F. Sarmiento identified it as an internal conflict between urban civilization and the barbarism of the gauchos. In the present century, on the other hand, it has been redefined as a struggle for the preservation of Argentina's economic, political, and cultural independence against imperialism and cosmopolitanism. Outstanding among the early exponents of this view was Ricardo Rojas, who developed it in a series of books running from *La restauración nacionalista* (1909) to *El profeta de la pampa* (1945), a biography of Sarmiento, whom Rojas admired and agreed with on most other issues. As time wore on the implications of the new view were developed, or contested, by a host of writers, and other controversies were added.

There was never a time when Argentina did not have a substantial group of historians who strove to maintain the ideal of objectivity. The climate of opinion was against them, however, especially after the economic crash of 1930 and the interjection of fascism, communism, and Peronism. A polemical character crept, if it did not rush, into most historical writing, whether it dealt with the May Doctrine, Rivadavia, Rosas, and the gauchos, or with education, the land system, stock raising, industrialization, and petroleum, not to mention political parties and foreign relations. Even foreign contributions to historical writing about Argentina, which came mainly from the United States and Britain, were not exempt.

Guides. An illuminating account of the development of historical writing about Argentina occupies most of Joseph R. Barager's "The Historiography of the Río de la Plata since 1830," *Hispanic American Historical Review,* XXXIX, No. 4 (November 1959), 588-642. Earlier and longer works on the subject are Rómulo D. Carbia's *Historia crítica de la historiografía argentina* (1925; rev. ed., 1940) and Enrique de Gandía's *Los estudios históricos en la Argentina* (1931).* In addition, many works published to 1953 are described in Arthur P. Whitaker's *The United States and Argentina* (Cambridge, Mass., 1954), pp. 254-262. Consequently, the following suggestions stress subsequent publications, though not to the exclusion of earlier works. Further references will be found in Robin A. Humphreys, *Latin American History. A Guide to Works on Latin America in English* (London, 1958), and the periodical publications listed at the end of this appendix.

General histories of Argentina. Among one-volume works in English, the best is Ysabel F. Rennie's *The Argentine Republic* (New York, 1945). The older standard works by F. A. Kirkpatrick and Ricardo Levene (as translated by William S. Robertson) have begun to date. George Pendle's *Argentina* (2nd ed., London, 1961), though very brief, provides an excellent introduction to the contemporary scene. Among older works in Spanish, Enrique de Gandía's *Historia de la república argentina en el siglo XIX* (1940) still holds its place. Noteworthy additions have been Ernesto Palacio's *Historia de la Argentina, 1515-1938* (1954), a good example of revisionism, and Gustavo Gabriel Levene's *La Argentina se hizo así* (1960), more balanced but lively, also attractively illustrated.

Among the many essays by Argentine writers interpreting Argentine history, by far the best is José Luis Romero's *Las ideas políticas en Argentina* (1946), now made available in an English translation of the third edition by Thomas F. McGann, under the title *A History of Argentine Political Thought* (Stanford, Cal., 1963). This is not, as one might expect, a systematic study of the subject indicated, but it is a brilliant essay by a leading intellectual and once politically active Socialist on the interplay between certain political ideas and the changing human environment in Argentina from colonial times to 1955. As a study of the ideas themselves, José Ingenieros, *La evolución de las ideas*

* Unless otherwise noted, all works in Spanish cited in this appendix were published in Buenos Aires.

argentinas (4 vols., 1937), still remains standard. Among other interpretative essays that should be read for a rounded view are those by Ricardo Rojas mentioned above and three from the astringent pen of Ezequiel Martínez Estrada, *Radiografía de la pampa* (1942), *Muerte y transfiguración de Martín Fierro* (2 vols., 1948), and *Qué es esto? Catalinaria* (1956). The extreme left-wing school is well represented by J. J. Hernández Arregui's *La formación de la conciencia nacional* (1930-1960) (1960).

Nationalism. The last-named work also represents one of the diverse currents of Argentina's burgeoning nationalism. At the other extreme, Catholic right-wing nationalism can be sampled in *Concepción católica de la política* (1961), by a secular priest, Julio Meinvielle. The previous development of Argentine nationalist thought is sketched in a chapter in Arthur P. Whitaker's *Nationalism in Latin America* (Gainesville, Fla., 1962). Manuel Gálvez' *Entre la novela y la historia. Recuerdos de la vida literaria* (1962) is the autobiography of a noted novelist and nationalist.

Political. Notable recent works include *Ideario de Mayo* (1960), a large and valuable collection of documents edited by Narciso Binayán; Thomas F. McGann's *Argentina, the United States, and the Inter-American System, 1880-1914* (Cambridge, Mass., 1957), especially important for the generation of 1880; John J. Johnson's *Political Change in Latin America: The Emergence of the Middle Sectors* (Stanford, Cal., 1958), which deals extensively with twentieth-century Argentina; and Carlos Ibarguren's *La historia que he vivido* (1955), a fascinating autobiography by a leading conservative intellectual and politician. A new party history is *El partido comunista en la política argentina* (1962), by Jorge A. Ramos.

Works of narrower scope include three on the end of the Perón period: *Nuestros vecinos argentinos* (Santiago, Chile, 1956), by the Chilean Alejandro Magnet, a sequel to his *Nuestros vecinos justicialistas* (9th ed., Santiago, 1955), the leading work on the Perón period; Arthur P. Whitaker's *Argentine Upheaval: Perón's Fall and the New Regime* (New York, 1956), and Mario Amadeo's *Ayer, Hoy, Mañana* (1956), which tells some of the inside story of the revolt of 1955. For the period since 1956 Felix Luna's *Diálogos con Frondizi* (1963), though an apologia, is illuminating.

Valuable earlier works include Emilio Ravignani's *Historia constitucional de la República Argentina* (3 vols., 1926-1927), Ricardo Zorraquín Becú's *El federalismo argentino* (1937), Carlos Sánchez Viamonte's *Historia institucional de Argentina* (Mexico, 1948), and three biographies in English: Ricardo Rojas' *San Martín, Knight of the Andes*, tr. Herschel Brickell (New York, 1945), J. C. J. Metford's *San Martín, the Liberator* (Oxford, 1950), and Allison W. Bunkley's *The Life of Sarmiento* (Princeton, 1952).

Economic and Social. The highly important contributions to Argentine social history that have been made since 1940 by Gino Germani and his associates in Buenos Aires are best represented by his *Política y sociedad en una época de transición* (1962). Kalman H. Silvert's penetrating and original study *The Conflict Society: Reaction and Revolution in Latin America* (New Orleans, 1961), deals extensively with Argentina. *Juan B. Justo y las luchas sociales en Argentina* (1956), by Dardo Cúneo, is a fresh and illuminating study of the founder of Argentine socialism. H. S. Ferns breaks new ground in the whole broad field covered by his *Britain and Argentina in the Nineteenth Century* (Oxford, 1960), which is based on British sources. Another significant pioneering work is *Entrepreneurship in Argentine Culture: Torcuato di Tella and S.I.A.M.* (Philadelphia, 1962), by Thomas C. Cochran and Ruben E. Reina. A broad and illuminating contemporary view is provided by Leopold Portnoy's *Análisis crítico de la economía argentina* (Mexico, D.F., 1961). Biased but still valuable accounts of two important issues are presented in *Historia de los ferrocarriles argentinos* (2d ed., 1958), by Raúl Scalabrini Ortiz, *Historia de los contratos petroleros* (1963), by Arturo Sábato, and *Economía y política del petróleo argentino* (1939-1956) (1957), by Marcos Kaplan. Raúl Larra's *Mosconi, general del petróleo* (1957) deals with the first director of Y.P.F. Much valuable information about the recent economic development of Argentina is contained in various reports of the Economic Commission for Latin America, an agency of the United Nations Economic and Social Council, and others prepared in the Pan American Union. Two important works of broader scope by Robert J. Alexander are *Communism in Latin America* (New Brunswick, 1957) and *Labor Relations in Argentina, Brazil, and Chile* (New York, 1962).

Older works that are still indispensable include Alejandro E. Bunge's *La economía argentina* (4 vols., 1928), Miron Burgin's *The Economic Aspects of Argentine Federalism, 1820-1852* (Cambridge, Mass., 1946), Simon G. Hanson's *Argentine Meat and the British Market* (Palo Alto, Cal., 1938), Vernon L. Phelps, *The International Economic Position of Argentina* (Philadelphia, 1938), Adolfo Dorfman, *Evolución industrial argentina* (1940), and Madaline W. Nichols, *The Gaucho* (Durham, N.C., 1942).

Literature and education. From the point of view of the present study, most of the important recent works in this category are of the interpretative variety already noted above. Only a few need be added here. The outpouring stimulated by the sesquicentenary of the May Revolution of 1810 is well represented by *Algunos aspectos de la cultura literaria de Mayo* (La Plata, 1960), a collection of articles published by the Departamento de Letras, Universidad Nacional de La Plata. The controversial University Reform of 1918 is lauded by one of its chief promoters, Gabriel del Mazo, in *Reforma universitaria y cultura nacional* (1955), a collection of his articles and addresses, with a prologue by Luis Alberto Sánchez. Problems at the school level are discussed in *Ideas pedagógicas del siglo XX* (1961), by Lorenzo Luzuriaga, and *La llamada crisis de la escuela activa* (1963), by E. Uzcátegui. A short but exceptionally valuable monograph by Angel Rosenblatt, *Las generaciones argentinas del siglo XIX ante el problema de la lengua* (1961), rejects the notion that *Martín Fierro* is a national epic and concludes that it is not only the elegy of the gaucho but a literary dead end. *Martín Fierro* is available in an English translation by Walter Owen (New York, 1936).

Still unrivalled in its field is Ricardo Rojas' *Historia de la literatura argentina* (6 vols., 1948, the latest of several editions).

Armed forces and the Catholic Church. The role of Argentina's armed forces is examined critically in Edwin Lieuwen's pioneering study, *Arms and Politics in Latin America* (rev. ed., New York, 1961). A broader and wholly favorable account of their role is given in *La historia patria y la acción de sus armas* (1960), published by the Círculo Militar Argentino as a special number of *Revista Militar*. A left-wing view is presented by Jorge Abelardo Ramos in *Historia política del ejército argentino* (1959). Two sympathetic studies of the Roman Catholic Church are John J. Kennedy's *Catholicism, Nationalism, and Democracy in Argentina* (University of Notre Dame, 1958), and *La doctrina católica en el desenvolvimiento constitucional argentino* (1957), by Miguel Angel Micheletti and others. Both deal mainly with the period since 1853, whereas the early national period is explored in Guillermo Gallardo's *La política religiosa de Rivadavia* (1962). The standard older work is Lloyd Mecham's *Church and State in Latin America* (Chapel Hill, N.C., 1934).

International Relations. Harold F. Peterson's *Argentina and the United States, 1810-1960* (New York, 1963) is the first comprehensive history of their diplomatic relations. Also comprehensive is *Historia de las conferencias interamericanas* (1959) by Enrique V. Corominas. E. Louise Peffer updates an old question in *Foot-and-Mouth Disease in*

United States Policy (Stanford, 1962, reprinted from *Food Research Institute Studies*, III, No. 2, May 1962). Argentine views on recent issues can be sampled in Arturo Frondizi's *La política exterior argentina* (1962), presidential addresses with a prologue by Dardo Cúneo, and Mario Amadeo's *Por una convivencia internacional* (1954). The best broad view of Argentina's oversea claims, both its perennial one to the Falkland Islands and its newer and more successful one in the Antarctic, is still provided by the Universidad Nacional de La Plata's *Soberanía argentina en el archipiélago de las Malvinas y en la Antártida* (La Plata, 1951), though Ricardo R. Caillet-Bois and others have subsequently illumined both themes. Recent works of broad international scope in which Argentina plays an important part include Donald R. Shea's *The Calvo Clause* (Minneapolis, 1955), J. Lloyd Mecham's *The United States and Inter-American Security* (Austin, 1961), and C. Neale Ronning's *Law and Politics in Inter-American Security* (New York, 1963).

Current. For current scholarly articles and reviews see the quarterly *Hispanic American Historical Review* and the annual *Handbook of Latin American Studies;* for monthly news digests, the *Hispanic American Report;* and for a rich assortment of statistical data, the annual *Statistical Abstract of Latin America,* published by the Center for Latin American Studies, University of California, Los Angeles. More detailed data are given in *América en cifras—1961* (Washington, D.C., n.d.) by the Inter-American Statistical Institute, Pan American Union.

INDEX

A.B.C. bloc, 64
Action Française, 80
Adams, John Quincy, 108
Africa, 2, 17
Agrarian reform, 12
Agriculture, 4, 5, 41, 42, 49, 51, 52-53, 74, 106, 123, 125, 126, 137, 149
Aguinaldo, 115
Air lines, 6
Albania, 111
Alberdi, Juan Bautista, 21, 30, 31, 34, 35, 43, 49
Alem, Leandro, 45, 46, 66, 69
Alfalfa, 51
Alliance for Progress, 2, 160, 169
Alvarez, Agustín, 59
Alvear, Marcelo T. de, 66, 77-79, 89, 96, 97
Amadeo, Mario, 144, 152
Anarchism, 45, 58, 74
Andes, 5, 24, 31, 35, 111
Anticlericalism, 26, 28, 43-44, 115, 141-144, 146, 147
Anti-Semitism, 13
Antipersonalist Radicals, 78-79, 89, 91, 96, 100
Aramburu, Pedro, 15, 144, 152-157, 164
Argentina, differentiated, 1-8; growth and stagnation, 2-3, 4-5, 124, 137, 168; name, 23, 37
Argentine Action, 102-103

Argentine Institute for the Promotion of Trade (IAPI), 123, 125
Argentine State Merchant Fleet, 137
Argentinidad, 62
Armed forces, 1, 10-12, 21, 23, 45, 46, 68, 72, 78, 80, 82, 83-88, 95, 100-103, 104-105, 107-110, 112, 114, 118-119, 129, 140, 142, 143-144, 146, 147-148, 151-157, 158-159, 163-167, 169
Arms control, 70
Artigas, José, 26
Asia, 2
Asociación de Mayo, see May Association
Assembly of 1813, 26
Asunción, 149
Authoritarianism, 1, 2, 21, 23, 87, 104
Avalos, Eduardo, 118
Avellaneda, Nicolás, 39, 59
Avenida de Mayo, 60
Axis, 101, 108, 116, 117

Bagú, Sergio, 75
Balance of power, 99, 107, 125
Balbín, Ricardo, 141, 158
Banco Central Argentino, 92, 153
Bank of England, 50, 92
Barbed wire, 51
Bariloche, 167
Baring Brothers, 50
Bases, book, 34
Becke, Carlos von der, 117

177